Château Latour

Christie's Wine Companion 2

Christie's Wine Companion 2

Edited by Patrick Matthews

Designed by Christopher Bradshaw FSIAD for
Christie's Wine Publications

Christie's Wine Publications
8 King Street, St James's, London SW1, England

Editor-in-chief Michael Broadbent, MW
Editor Patrick Matthews

ISBN 0 903432 30 7

Printed in England by
Eyre & Spottiswoode Ltd, Queen's Printers,
at Grosvenor Press, Portsmouth

Contents

Introduction

I am very happy to introduce our second *Wine Companion*, confidently trusting that the variety of content will afford as much delightful reading as that of the first.

Although we did not announce that the Christie's *Wine Companion* published in the autumn of 1981, was the first of a series, this was certainly our intention though had our readers not taken to it we would, of course, have thought again. Was this just faint-hearted or prudent? I am always mildly amused when our friends across the water, and I do not refer to the English Channel, boldly announce 'the first annual' charity wine auction, 'first annual international exposition,' 'grand seminar' and so forth. As our forebears put it, bluntly: 'fools rush in . . . .'

But surely we cannot go wrong with a roll-call of writers and artists such as ours, which include, at random Jack Plumb, a great stylist, formidable academic, and a 'wine amateur' in the grand tradition; Alice, Hugo Dunn-Meynell's wife, with a vignette of the quality which takes me back to the first *Journal* of the Wine & Food Society – what stature the contributors were in those days; the doyens of wine writing and wine tasting respectively – Eddie Penning-Rowsell and Harry Waugh; the personal experience of two rather contrasting authors in the wine field, *our* Peter Sichel, as opposed to the cousin in New York; and that gulper of life, Max Lake.

In this issue we have a bevy of the relatively new yet firmly established professionals in the field of wine writing: David Peppercorn and his wife and fellow Master of Wine, Serena Sutcliffe; Bob Thompson and Burton Anderson, whose knowledge of wine and wine makers in their respective fields, California and Italy, is encyclopaedic and, even more important, whose judgement is sound.

We also have the *enfant terrible* of Burgundy, Anthony Hanson, whose controversial book certainly provoked thought, amongst other reactions; Jancis Robinson, representing all that wine writers should be and sometimes aren't, describes her experiences making the first serious series on wine for television in this country. My very old friend and direct counterpart at Sotheby's contributes a pen portrait of a great man of wine from the Cape. And, no introduction needed, there is Hugh Johnson, the title of whose latest book bears an uncanny similarity to ours – but we forgive him.

A word about the artists. Charles Mozley is a brilliant draughtsman and colourist. He works at lightning speed yet every line is exactly right. In the first *Wine Companion* we reprinted some of his deliciously witty, wicked and occasionally erotic drawings. Here we reproduce equally vivid and idiosyncratic lithographic portraits of Bordeaux *châteaux* and vineyards, part of a series published by Christie's in 1975 and now very much collectors' pieces. There are also examples of old prints, often cruelly outspoken, always pointed, with subject matter explained by collector, dealer and one-time member of Christie's wine department, Jeremy Roberts.

Last but not least, I should like to thank Patrick Matthews, who has, with patience and charm, selected, commissioned, cajoled and assembled the contents, and Christopher Bradshaw who has presented them visually for our delectation. I very much hope that what they have combined to produce will feast the eyes, provide food for thought, and entertain.

Michael Broadbent, MW
Christie's, Autumn 1983

Colette and wine
Alice Wooledge Salmon

I was very well brought up. As first proof of such a statement, I'll tell you I was no more than three when my father offered me a glassful of the sun-burnt wine from his native Midi: le muscat de Frontignan.

Illumination, capsizing of the senses, revelation for the taste buds! This baptism made me wine's worthy convert. A little later, I learned to drain my tumbler of mulled wine, perfumed with lemon and cinnamon, while dining off boiled chestnuts. Hardly able to read, I spelled out each drop of aging and graceful bordeaux rouges and dazzling Yquem. Then came the murmuring froth of champagne, springing in pearls of air across birthday and first communion banquets to celebrate the grey truffles of la Puisaye . . . A good education, from which I progressed to judicious familiarity with wine, never gulped and swilled, but measured into slim glasses and absorbed by sips at reflective intervals.

Colette presents her credentials, the same Colette who died a French monument, had a state funeral, and is famous in many languages for extreme love of animals and flawless writing about wayward, ambiguous men and women.

The most casual reading of three or four of her 50-odd books and sheaves of essays proclaims that Colette was *gourmande*, emotionally attached to large loaves of crusty bread and hand-pressed butter, lacquer-red cherries, honeyed

Colette, by Jean Cocteau

figs, and the slow-cooking dishes of rural Burgundy, their secrets whispered among housewives at vinous country weddings and rarely recorded. She loved cheese, water chestnuts, and a bewitching old *daube* from Provence which simmered beef, bacon, and garlic with 'oil that lurks in the sauce and wine which gives it splendour, a special fragrance'.

Many pages and a fair amount of nonsense have been written about Colette and her marriages, numerous liaisons, and career in the music-hall, the notoriety that with age turned to fame and adulation. Her life was extraordinary, her personality lacking in banality to a degree which most people would find hard to tolerate – 'You can't imagine what it's like to live with a woman who is always barefoot', said her second husband – and just as one's pleasure in rare wine can be blunted by undue dissection, so various critics have taken Colette to absurdities in their haste after 'psychoanalysis' of both woman and achievement.

Not so the Burgundian oenologist and wine writer Pierre Poupon, who by way of endorsing her vinous credentials simply judges Colette 'our most perceptive wine writer' and suggests that the Collège de France should have named her *professeur de Dégustation*: 'Her works ought to be the bedside books of professional and amateur tasters, to their much greater benefit than all those pages which preach the mechanics of tasting and never divulge the spirit'[1].

In 1951, Pierre Poupon was secretary and member of the *jury* in charge of awarding the *prix littéraire* at the Paulée de Meursault, one of 'three glorious' November feasts which celebrate the Burgundy vintage; that year Colette was chosen for the excellence of her Burgundian writings and the particular essay *Ma Bourgogne pauvre* She neglected to accept this distinction, and many startled inhabitants of la Maison de Vieux Artistes Retraités de Ris-Orangis were soon delighting in the contents of 100 bottles of Meursault that should have been her recompense.

Well, I said she was extraordinary. It was Sido, Colette's mother and inspiration, who taught her to 'divine the hidden treasure' in every aspect of the physical world through fullest employment of the five senses, of which the 'noblest, most lucid and uncompromising' became to Colette the sense of smell. Folded away in the 1870s and '80s at Saint-Sauveur-en-Puisaye, a market town near Auxerre in the Basse-Bourgogne, 'bereft of vines' save for some light-hearted *vin de Treigny* whose stock did not resist phylloxera, the child shot up

---

[1] Pierre Poupon, *'Colette, ou l'art de la dégustation'*, *Mes Dégustations littéraires*, Nuits-Saint-Georges, 1979.

nimble and receptive, her intuition schooled to the significance of *'le monde matériel, sphérique, bondé de saveurs'*. Lessons well-learned; one fragment of a sentence from the autobiographical *Maison de Claudine* engages all alert senses: 'the echoing house, dry, warm and crackling as a newly-baked loaf'.

And Sido contributed some *grands crus*, vintage pre-phylloxera, to that 'good education'. As antidote to the possibility of adolescent pallors, Colette was given unusual tonics: from the dry sand of her granite *cave*, Sido unearthed bottles she had hidden from invading Germans at the time of the Franco-Prussian war, '. . . wine left by my first husband. Château-Larose, Château-Lafite, Chambertin, Château-Yquem. Bottles already ten, twelve, fifteen years old (at the moment of burial). That good dry sand made them even better', and glass after glass escorted Colette's afternoon *casse-croûte* of cutlet or cold chicken as Sido watched her cheeks flame with the 'vinous glories of France'.

Colette grew up to write ripe, full-bodied prose, savoury with archaic words and racy dialogue, prose which 'improves with age like wines that grow rich in the bottle', as well-described by Pierre Poupon. The vineyard and *cru* appear so often in her work – a rapid mention, a chapter, the metaphor for complex emotions – that the present tasting must be highly selective.

Three essays form the heart of this writing. *Vins* is based on that vinous education, *En Bourgogne* evokes Burgundian cellars in winter, and *Ma Bourgogne pauvre*, the prize winner, moves from childhood wines to the Côte d'Or. The three overlap, as so often occurs with Colette, and reveal qualities of *vigneron* and *caviste* that complement the taster.

She felt wine as a great mystery, but attentive, she learned secrets: its different translations of the soil's 'true flavour', the tastes of flint or chalk or that of a *sauvignon* graft from Bordeaux which sugared and lightened Algerian wine of quite another character.

She sensed that sap quickened in the sleeping vine of a stripped winter vineyard despite all visual evidence, marvelled at snake-like *provençal* stock apparently nourished by dew alone, and observed grapes, 'clear and cloudy agate or silver-dusted blue' as a fine summer brought them to splendid maturity.

Tasting wines *sur place*, finding six bottles of Jurançon – 'fiery, imperious prince, treacherous as all great seducers' – at a village auction taught Colette more geography than any professor, just as 'glorious' wine once drunk in a dark old inn delighted her like the stolen kiss of an unseen stranger.

She was soothed by winter industry in the cellars of an *éleveur* where one man racked wine, another fined it by rocking a *dodine* to distribute egg white, and a third scoured casks by means of heavy chain. Here was quiet, rhythmic work, in

The Grand Véfour

no particular hurry, whose midwifery brought forth 'His Royal Highness the Wine of Burgundy' on which she'd been raised but whose Côte d'Or she never knew till much later. It was a case of love at first sight. 'My initial visit, at the height of a glowing September, the hills all laden with their vintage, landed me in a Dijon which local festivities, the hot Indian summer and its jollifications had set alight, ashamed neither of being rich nor of lavishing the treasures of a city given over to gastronomic pleasure and running with eternities of wine.'

Translation is hard on Colette's sumptuous, multi-layered vocabulary and pell-mell of images, the words chosen for their exact and often double or triple meanings. The following sentence from *Ma Bourgogne pauvre* shows why she gains when read in the original: '*La veine qui charrie les crus illustres passe assez loin de la Puisaye, bifurque puis tarit*'. The word *veine*, in French, indicates both 'vein' or 'seam' and 'underground stream'; *charrier* means to 'bear' or 'carry' and is often associated with transport on rivers; *bifurquer*, to 'fork' or 'divide', applies equally to seam or road and to stream; and *tarir* means to 'dry up', 'cease', or 'peter out'. Four words which give both a geological concept – the 'seam' of soil and subsoil that bears and nourishes the great wines of the Côte d'Or – and the idea of a hidden river, even a source or a spring, one of Colette's symbols of the life force with which, by inference, wine is allied. Translation to 'The seam that bears the illustrious growths passes nowhere near la Puisaye, divides and then peters out' must sacrifice the second meaning.

But often the message arrives. In *Vins*, Colette evokes a 'violet-perfumed bordeaux', colour of the '*rubis balais*' or balas ruby, a rose-red variety from north-eastern Persia near Samarkand. That's quite an image; not just 'ruby', but arrayed with connotations both specific and exotic, bringing all sorts of echoes, pipe dreams of adventure to the well-regulated slopes of the Gironde.

And now let's roam. Colette is first-rate on *vendanges*, grape-pickings in the Beaujolais, the Limousin, and Provence – where for 12 years or so she owned vines that yielded up to 2,000 litres a season. *Automne* brings the whole department of the Var out to 'save' the grapes of a vintage whose clusters trail on the burning August earth; the women sing, their voices carried by the wind from Mediterranean gulf to gulf, drunken and defenceless wasps fall about sticky vats, and folk in all sorts of kitchens boil the new wine to make into *vin marquis*. *Mon amie Valentine* sits down to a large harvest lunch: *la soupe, poule au pot*, pork 'pink and white as a breast, veal in its goodness'. In September 1941, gripped by wartime shortage, Colette encouraged readers of her newspaper column to reflect on the coming vintage, the autumn sun which stimulates late-ripening grapes, and the lure of good bottles, for the moment empty but as ready to put

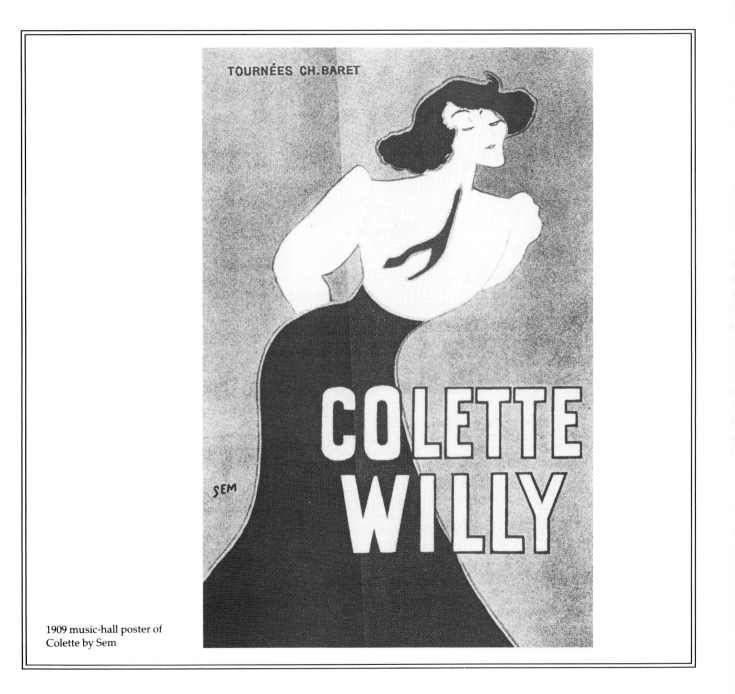

1909 music-hall poster of
Colette by Sem

up 'the tomato and the *haricot vert'* as to welcome fresh wine (*De ma fenêtre*). And much of *La Naissance du jour*, an essay-like novel about renunciation in middle age, is based on the *vendange* as a metaphor for the culmination and reflective aftermath of love, gathered up and put aside to slumber in the memory like the 'cloistered new wine'.

Colette's voice, with its rugged and rolling Burgundian 'r', spoke of wine as both intoxicant – like opium, perfume, silk and velvet, the music of speech, sexual love, all the *'enivrant superflu'* – and a symbol of restraint: 'And drink little, if you don't mind. We have a saying, where I come from, that during a good meal one isn't thirsty but "hungry to drink" '. Not just restraint, but positive order and sometimes elegance, even among marginal people, the 'bourgeois bohemia' who were Colette's recurring subjects. If she alluded to *lorettes* – the rank and file of Parisian kept women, circa 1840 – as drawn by Gavarni with 'shoulders in the shape of Rhine wine bottles', and to fusty, political, all-male luncheons washed down in dim restaurants with Richebourg and other oh-so-respectable growths, she used champagne as a kind of passe-partout. Weddings and birthdays – her 75th brought a jeroboam – New Year's *réveillon*, courtship (honourable and otherwise), a moment of ambiguity were refreshed with Piper-Heidsieck, a good *brut* of 1906, a Pommery, or – not so successfully – a night-club brew 'that tastes metallic'.

Pommery is the champagne of Colette's to me best-realised creation: Léa de Lonval, courtesan of the *belle époque* and light of *Chéri* and *La Fin de Chéri*, stories of the sentimental education and extinction of Chéri, *'jeune homme riche au petit coeur'*. Léa, handsomely 50, has 'kept' the boy, aged 25, for seven years; they part, he marries, and in losing each other both relinquish the finest possession either will ever have. It's a world of money, love, and small curiosity, as respectable as milieux less irregular, and Léa, whose career has been sure-footed and profitable, is a woman of great if somewhat hot-house style.

'Elle aimait l'ordre, le beau linge, les vins mûris, la cuisine réfléchie' – She liked order, good linen, wine that has mellowed and well-considered cooking.' She lunches alone, 'with a smile for the dry Vouvray and the June strawberries, served with their stalks on a Rubelles plate, green as a tree-frog after the rain'; the dining room assimilates Louis XVI mirrors, English furniture of the same period, heavy silver, and a butler whose 'restrained glance' announces *'Madame est belle'* and does not displease her. Léa's *eau-de-vie*, refined by seven decades, is poured from cut-glass into goblets of the thinnest crystal, served with iced water and shortbread biscuits on a cloth of old embroidery.

But it's Pommery which signifies the essence that Chéri, grieving and rudderless, can't bear to lose. 'And he breathed in, remembering, as he opened his nostrils, the rose-perfumed sparkle of an old champagne of 1889 that Léa kept for him alone.' Chéri, whom Léa had mocked as a *petit bourgeois* when he counted up her bottles, tells her at the end of volume one, 'In the very wine I drank I looked for you, and never found a Pommery like yours', before they part finally with bittersweet sorrow.

Appropriately, Colette spent her last 16 years in the rue de Beaujolais in Paris, dying there, aged 81, 'after a small sip of champagne'. Three of her windows, on the first floor of the graceful Palais-Royal, overlooked the semi-private world of its gardens, and her final handful of years, when she was crippled with arthritis and never out of pain, were cheered by the proximity of the Grand Véfour, restaurant returned to quality in the late 1940s by Raymond Oliver. Colette and husband made it their 'local', met friends, entertained there, and as she couldn't walk, Oliver used to have her collected by two liveried waiters and a sedan chair. Her favourite Véfour lunch was salmon *coulibiac* – with champagne, *bien sûr*.

A final word from Colette? 'A difficult page, the conclusion of a novel, are advantageously served by an exceptionally well-filled glass.'

Colette Willy

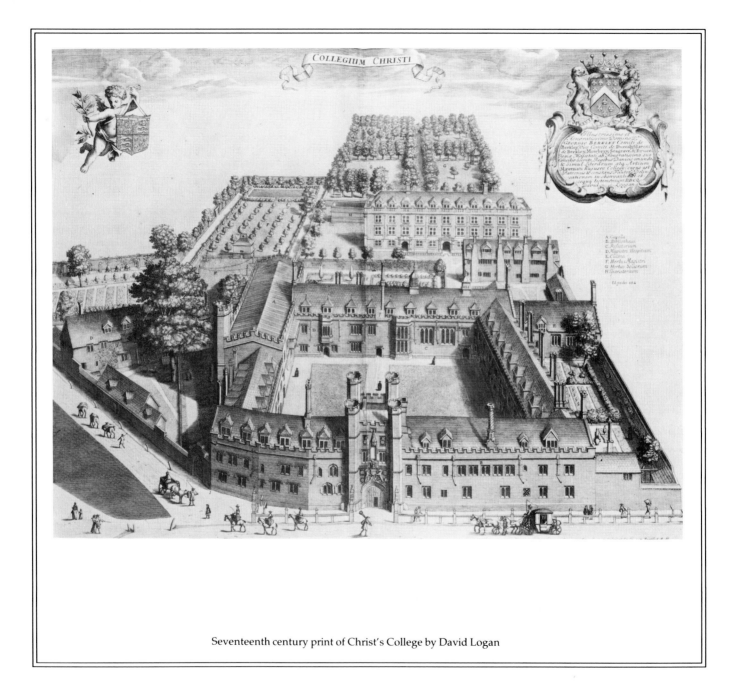

Seventeenth century print of Christ's College by David Logan

Saintsbury 1982 *Sir John Plumb*

Dons at Oxford and Cambridge began to club together in the middle of the 18th century to buy wine and drink together – to combine, as they called it, after dinner, which was then eaten at about four o'clock in the afternoon. During the long evenings, as well as drinking they played cards; sometimes they sang glees or played music together in their garden. In most colleges, these activities are no longer run like a club but have been taken over by the college as a corporate activity. At Christ's College, Cambridge, however, the senior cellar is still run independently of the college, 'the members of the room' being responsible entirely for its finances and for the way matters are conducted. In the 19th century, the fellows of Christ's also ran their own garden in a similar way. At Christ's the wine books, which account for every bottle of wine drunk in the Room since the mid-1780s, still exist. They show that a very keen interest was taken in fine wines and from earliest times many fellows had their own private cellars. After dons were allowed to marry, these drinking habits flourished in private houses as well as colleges, and George Saintsbury's *Notes on a Cellar Book* give a clear picture of the professional round of wining and dining in Edinburgh in the late 19th and early 20th centuries. The wine books give us a similar insight.

Dons at Oxford, Cambridge, Edinburgh and elsewhere live today in a much diminished world; and our habits of entertainment would have perplexed Saintsbury. I am sure that he would have been distressed to find ladies dressed in corduroy trousers, gentlemen without ties or with shirts open to the navel, at a dinner party. He would have been perplexed by his hostess dashing into the kitchen during the meal and serving the courses which she brought back. And, of course, the shortness of the meal would have baffled him. Saintsbury and his wife usually provided between eight and ten courses at their dinners – today three are usual; perhaps at a college lodge one might still get four. Saintsbury, however, was no conservative; indeed, in food and drink he was adventurous, even trying 'a pullet sperm in the brewage' during a walk on Skye. As an undergraduate, he drank Bishop, a mulled wine even then rapidly disappearing from the repertoire of Oxford and Cambridge colleges. And he devoted a vacation to the search for white beer in Cornwall and Devon, but it proved as elusive as the unicorn. So he would have taken today's Chilean Cabernet and white wines from the remoter reaches of Yugoslavia or Bulgaria in his stride. Doubtless he would have sampled with curiosity and some wonderment English wines, whose possibility he regarded as a huge joke in bad taste. But at the end of the meal, when he would have been very lucky to get a crusted port, let alone a vintage one, he would have felt very thirsty. Saintsbury thought a bottle of white and a bottle of red per person good average drinking. Today at Oxford and Cambridge such drinking at dinner would be – in most don's homes – regarded as Bacchanalian dissipation. Although the food would be well below the standards he grew to expect in quantity, he would, I think, have been delighted by its variety – the avocado pears, the fennel, the aubergines, the red and green peppers, which most dons' wives take for granted. Also the standard of cooking can be very high indeed; not always but sometimes.

Fortunately for the ghost of Saintsbury, there are still oases of fine drinking in Cambridge and Oxford and perhaps elsewhere but, even in these, customs now prevail which might strike him as odd. I am happy to say that my own college is one of these oases; and a very historically minded one. We have never allowed fellows to purchase wine from the cellar to take home – it has to be drunk with other fellows and their guests in the Room. It has had only three wine stewards, complete autocrats, and no committee, to buy wine during this century. It also has a very close connection indeed with George Saintsbury and his *Cellar Book*.

Sidney Grose, my tutor and predecessor as wine steward of Christ's College, who died recently at the ripe age of 94, had begun to take an interest in fine wine when he returned to the college in the early 1920s but his imagination was really fired in the early summer of 1927. Let me quote from his own first cellar book, dated 9 Aug 1927: 'The idea of keeping an account of my wine had matured during the last few weeks after reading George Saintsbury's, a copy of which has been given me by my pupil, Douglas Clark, our organist.' But there was also a member of the college, Valentine Richards, the dean of the college and wine steward, more or less a contemporary of Saintsbury, who was as passionately concerned with fine wine as Saintsbury, and a man who was remarkably generous to his colleagues. As Grose wrote: 'I could hardly start under better auspices, but Valentine Richards and George Saintsbury reach heights to which I cannot aspire.' He was too modest; by 1929 he had a splendid cellar – 20 dozen fine claret, most of it first growths, including four splendid double magnums of Mouton-Rothschild 1924, of which, some 30 years later, he gave me two, for Grose initiated me into fine claret and fine wine. The first bottle of Lafite I ever possessed, a '20, was given to me by him at 7.30 am one summer morning in 1932 when I took his daughter back after the college ball. After the war in the late 40s, he asked me if I would consider taking over some time as wine steward. I agreed and 21 years later he thought my apprenticeship might come to an end and that all would not be lost if he handed over the cellar to my keeping. Indeed, he handed over a magnificent cellar – still a few '20s – particularly Latour '28, but some Lafite '29 and also the delicious Ducru-Beaucaillou of the same vintage. Some great burgundies of the '23 vintage, particularly Chambertin and, above all, wonderful Sauternes; a bottle or two of 1878 La Tour Blanche and more bottles still of the Yquem '21 which had been laid down by Valetine Richards – alas, now all drunk. Another splendid Valentine Richards purchase was the Montrachet 1911 which still drank superbly even in the late 50s. It was a great inheritance. But so were the records for the wine books which stretched back nearly two centuries; and equally fascinating were the menus carefully collected by Grose of all the important dinners in college. They reached back to before World War I.

What is immediately clear is that Professor Saintsbury's way of life was far from unique. What was unique about Saintsbury was his enthusiasm to write about it: then he was an obsessive author. If we compare Valentine Richards's cellar with Saintsbury's, it is obvious that Valentine Richards had bottles of greater age; probably he possessed a broader range of fine wines and his great old vintages were more carefully husbanded than Saintsbury's. Of course, until he became professor at Edinburgh, Saintsbury was very peripatetic, whereas Valentine Richards lived his long life at Christ's and nowhere else. Also, he had the use of a magnificent cellar, dry and cold. We learn most about Valentine Richards's cellar from his benefactions to the Senior Combination Room recorded in the wine books. Unfortunately some of the entries in the wine books merely state that Valentine Richards presented a bottle of claret, or port or champagne or Sauternes from his own cellar, without naming the growth or vintage. There are many entries, however, that are complete. He gave the following wines in the early 1920s: ports, 1847, '51, '63, '68, '78, '84, 1900, '08, '12, not once but many times, and his resources must have been large for in 1932 he thought that the 1851 was drinking particularly well and presented five bottles of it in rapid succession. (There may have been a darker reason; he was becoming increasingly unwell in 1932 – he died early in 1933 – and he may not have wanted to leave the '51 behind.) He donated the following clarets: Margaux 1869 and 1914; Léoville 1870, 1914; La Mission-Haut-Brion 1893, 1905; Gruaud-Larose 1914; Giscours 1920; Ausone 1923. The last bottle he presented was a bottle of Léoville-Poyferré 1870 in 1932. Madeira was a frequent gift, particularly his 1820 Bual and the 1874 Sercial. Of Sauternes, of which the college has always been very fond, largely due to Valentine Richards, he gave the Yquem 1884 on innumerable occasions as well as Yquem 1914, '17 and '21. From other sources (Grose bought a number of his wines when he died) we know that he had very fine old sherries (1874 in particular), huge quantities of champagne, which he liked drinking old. In the 1920s he was drinking the 1898. He bought the 1921 hocks very heavily, which the Room purchased when he died. They adorned every college feast throughout the 30s. His burgundies were comprehensive and his claret cellar far far larger than his gifts would lead one to believe. For example, Grose speaks in 1931 of Valentine Richards's wonderful bin of 1899 Château Latour.

And Valentine Richards believed, like Saintsbury, that fine wine demanded fine glass: he formed a wonderful collection of old glass now in the Fitzwilliam Museum, a collection of wine glasses and decanters worthy of his wine. I suspect that Valentine Richards's cellar may be the greatest possessed by a don of this century both in breadth and depth. But it was by no means a solitary peak. His colleague Dr Barclay of Christ's could rival him in port. There were fellows of Trinity, St John's and King's who could dine and wine Valentine Richards as well as he could them and often did. It was the range and quantity of his wines that put him ahead.

Going through the wine books and menus of my college has revealed other surprises. It was a very conservative college in its eating and drinking habits – the number and style of courses at a formal college feast did not change from before 1900 to World War II – always nine courses with dessert. This was about the same number of courses that Saintsbury gave to his guests on a special occasion. How they managed to eat so much baffles my understanding. However, their drinking habits were even more unlike our own. In May 1925, for example, they drank three wines with their nine courses: La Ina sherry, Pfälzer Traminer Auslese 1911, Louis Roederer 1914. Only after dinner did they turn to red, when they drank Lafite 1899, 1857 port and Old Bual madeira. White wine with dinner, red after: this had always been the custom as far back as we can trace, certainly back into the 19th century.[1] There was a revolution on 14 May 1929 when a burgundy – a Chambertin 1915 – was offered as an alternative to the Deidesheimer Hofstück 1921. At the next feast, the conservative party in the college won and the burgundy was dropped, but in the late 1930s the forces of progress firmly triumphed and a burgundy, as a substitute for champagne, was served for the next three decades. Only in the late 1960s did I, with trepidation, serve a claret at a feast with the food – probably the first time in the college's history.

Often visitors are surprised to find us drinking claret after dinner, night after night, but it is a very old custom of many Oxford and Cambridge colleges. The fellows of old loved their claret much more than port. But they had curious addictions. They drank nothing but 1914 Gruaud-Larose for over five years and, when that was finished, they turned to Château Latour 1978, which lasted for three years. And yet the cellar was teeming with different growths and different vintages – massive quantities of the 1920 or '24, let alone earlier years. The members of the Room today demand greater variety, although occasionally we have long runs.

In the careful hands of Valentine Richards and Sidney Grose, inspired by Saintsbury, the college cellar has been, and I like to think will be, worthy of the college traditions for the rest of this century. It is still strong in Sauternes as Valentine Richards would have wished, yet no Yquem has been bought since the 50s. Although we have some first growths of claret – up to 1962 – that is the end of them; the price now is far too high. The ports, however, march majestically on from the 1927s to the 1977s in large quantities – due partly to some very generous benefactions. The great white burgundies alas are too dear – no young fellow will have my education in them. I was weaned as a wine drinker on Le Montrachet 1911, a very noble wine. Fine hocks and moselles we

---

[1] It may have derived from the usual habits of dining amongst the upper middle class – red wine stains the teeth so maybe it was only drunk after the ladies had withdrawn. If so, it is odd that this persisted in a purely male society. Also, Trollope writes of red wine being drunk at dinner. So it is an open question.

A knowledgeable company and fine wines – Sidney Grose, Neil Broderick, Sir John Plumb & C. P. Snow

can still manage, but one wonders for how long. Even bourgeois growths of claret have found their way into the Combination Room; that would not have disturbed Saintsbury, who took great delight in Château Citran thinking it far better than many fourth and fifth growths. Bourgeois wines are not yet served at feasts at my college, but inevitably they will be. And they, too, may become too expensive for a don's pocket. One has only to look at the menus of college feasts in Oxford as well as in Cambridge of the 30s or 50s compared with those of today. In recent years I have been given non-vintage port at a very grand college, and clarets scarcely known to *Cocks et Feret* at some of the poorer or more feckless colleges.

All is not gloom. There are one or two young fellows with very fine, large cellars of their own; wine-tasting societies flourish amongst the undergraduates and, at most times, they taste reasonable wines, occasionally good ones. There are endless wine tastings of raw wines, given by wine merchants, which I cannot believe does much good but, at least, it is a primary education. Valentine Richards and Sidney Grose put their trust in their wine merchants, particularly Harveys and Averys, not in their own capacity to distinguish year-old wines, yet their palates were fine and better exercised than most palates today.

In addition to the drinking of fine wines in college, both Oxford & Cambridge have proliferated with private dining clubs, some like *The Society* at Cambridge of great antiquity, where the dedicated lovers of fine wine and food could get together. Sidney Grose was a member of *The Society*, as was Valentine Richards. Here is the dinner they gave in Christ's on Monday 24 October 1927.

THE SOCIETY

———

Lundi, le 24 Octobre 1927

———

Huîtres au Naturel

———

Consommé Royale

———

Filets de Soles à la Normande

———

Mousse de Jambon

———

Hachis de Chevreuil

———

Canard Sauvage rôti
Salade Japonnaise

———

Petits Soufflés à la Fédora

———

Champignons sur Croûtes

———

Dessert

Sherry – Margarita
Marcobrunner Cabinet 1904
Clicquot 1911
Cockburn's 1878 port
Château Lafite 1878
Bristol Cream, bottled 1914

This would be difficult, perhaps impossible, to match today.

Château Haut-Brion
Edmund Penning-Rowsell

If seniority is of any account then Château Haut-Brion should be the first of the *premiers crus de Bordeaux* because it is certainly the oldest as a wine estate and possibly as an integrated property. For while there are ancient manorial records of the estates that later became Lafite and Latour, the remote parts of the Médoc were not the likely area for a seat of the Bordeaux aristocracy until the beginning of the 17th century and, more invitingly, after it had been drained by Dutch engineers in the middle of that century. On the other hand, the Graves, in which Bordeaux itself stands, was the original *Bordelais* vineyard, which gradually spread outward from the city. The oldest named vineyard is surely Pape-Clément, named after Bertrand de Goth, archbishop of Bordeaux, who in 1306 became Pope Clement V, and left his vineyard, which today is claimed to have been created in 1300, to the archbishop of Bordeaux and his successors. Château Pape-Clément is not far away from Haut-Brion and in the same *commune* of Pessac. Much of the fine *château* of Haut-Brion was built in 1550.

The era of the Pontacs Although the first-known proprietor of Haut-Brion was Jean de Ségur, who owned it in 1509, the first family associated with the property as a wine-producing estate was the Pontacs, whose name later on was often used for Haut-Brion itself, as well as denoting a wine of the Graves. Jean de Pontac, born in 1488, acquired Haut-Brion in the village of Pessac, when in 1525 he married Jeanne de Bellon, daughter of the mayor of Libourne, who brought it as part of her dowry. It was he who built the *château*, lived to the age of 101, and was said to be the richest man in Bordeaux. His grandson, Geoffrey de Pontac, inherited Haut-Brion; when he died in 1649 he left it to his elder son, Arnaud de Pontac, who, four years later, became first president of the *parlement* of Bordeaux, a complex of law courts rather than a political body, although it did have certain political powers. From here stemmed, as in other *parlements* in France, the *noblesse de robe*, so called because of their legal attire, who succeeded, at least in wealth, the *noblesse d'épée*. In 1663 Arnaud de Pontac's income was officially given as 25,000 *livres* (almost equivalent to francs, introduced at the Revolution). As the legal fees of the *parlement* were not high, this enormous income – in today's money probably a six-figure total – will have derived largely from property, including Haut-Brion, as was the case in the following century of the Marquis Nicholas-Alexandre Ségur, who owned Lafite, Latour, what later became Mouton and Calon-Ségur. The Pontac town house, the Maison Daurade, was the grandest private house in Bordeaux.

Arnaud de Pontac was not just the owner of Haut-Brion, which, as explained later, was far larger than it is today. He was interested in viticulture and it is claimed that he realised the importance of keeping the *barriques* topped up in order to age the wines, which he thought vital. It is impossible to determine when Haut-Brion was first marketed under that name, but it is certain that it was before the Médoc first growths were known. For it is now generally accepted that the vineyards of Lafite, Latour and Château Margaux were started as 'estate wines' about 1670, whereas there is the well-known entry in Samuel Pepys's diary on 10 April 1663 at the Royal Oak Tavern in London '. . . and there I drank a sort of French wine called Ho-Bryan which hath a good and most particular taste which I have never encountered. . .'. From this it may be inferred that this wine was produced from a mature vineyard of 20 or more years old, the product of Arnaud de Pontac's researches.

It may be thought that the first printed reference to Haut-Brion and the other *premiers crus* would have appeared and be available today in French rather than English sources. But this merely illustrates the fact that the only market for these superior, expensive wines lay among Britain's rich peers and middle classes, who, after the defeat of the Dutch, were now entering into a period of great prosperity as the leading merchants and traders of the existing world.

So in 1666 Arnaud's son, François-Auguste, opened in London a tavern significantly called 'The Sign of Pontac's Head'. The cook came from the Pontac mansion in Bordeaux and some at least of the wines must have come from Haut-Brion. Defoe, Dryden and Swift were all part of the clientele and mentioned it in their writings. The name of this inn probably contributed to the rather indiscriminate use of Pontac for Haut-Brion and even for other clarets from the Graves.[1]

English admirers

That Haut-Brion had a considerable reputation in this period may be judged from the comments of a distinguished Englishman, who, when in Bordeaux, went out of his way to visit the village of Pessac to see the source of the wine already well-known in England. On 14 May 1677 John Locke, the philosopher, recorded in his *Journal*:

'I rode out amongst other things saw President Pontac's vineyard at Hautbrion. It is a little rise of ground, lieing open most to the west. It is noe thing but pure, white sand mixed with a little gravell. One would imagine it scarce fit to bear any thing. Some of the vines are about 4 or 5 foot high and have stakes. Others are direct along the ground, not above a foot from it, between little, low stakes or laths, soe that the old branches stand on each side the root like a pair of armes spread out towards the south. The reason of this different way of culture I could not learne of the work men for want of understanding Gascon. This ground may be esteemed to yeild about 25 tuns of wine. However, the owner makes a shift to make every vintage 50, which he sells 100 *ecus*[2] per tun. It was sold some years since for 60, but the English love to raise the market on themselves. This however, they say & that men of skill & credit, that the wine in the very next vinyard, though in all things seeming equall to me, is not soe good.'

[1] It is very difficult to ascertain whether or not Pontac was an alternative 'general' name for Haut-Brion. Sometimes, as above, it seems to be a different wine, sometimes not. Locke's references seem to indicate that they were the same, Evelyn's that they were different but produced in the same vineyard. The later advertisements appear to suggest either way, but when Pontac is advertised alongside Margaux in the *London Gazette* (as in May 1705) it appears to be on a comparative 'first-growth' level. Moreover, in a letter in October 1723 from a merchant or agent in Bordeaux, J. Bruvenal, to the representative of the Prince of Wales, he refers to 'the 4 topping growths of La Tour, Lafite, Château Margaux and Pontac are exceeding good'. (The full letter is on page 107 of my *The Wines of Bordeaux*, London 1969). Surely someone living in Bordeaux would know when correctly retailing the names of the three top wines of the Médoc.

[2] One *ecu* was worth three *livres*, which were nearly equivalent to francs. One pound was worth 13 *livres* at this period. A crown = five shillings. In the 18th century the crown was taken as the rough equivalent of the *ecu*. The *livre* was roughly equal to the franc which superseded it at the Revolution. To secure an up-to-date equivalent it must be multiplied at least tenfold, if not more.

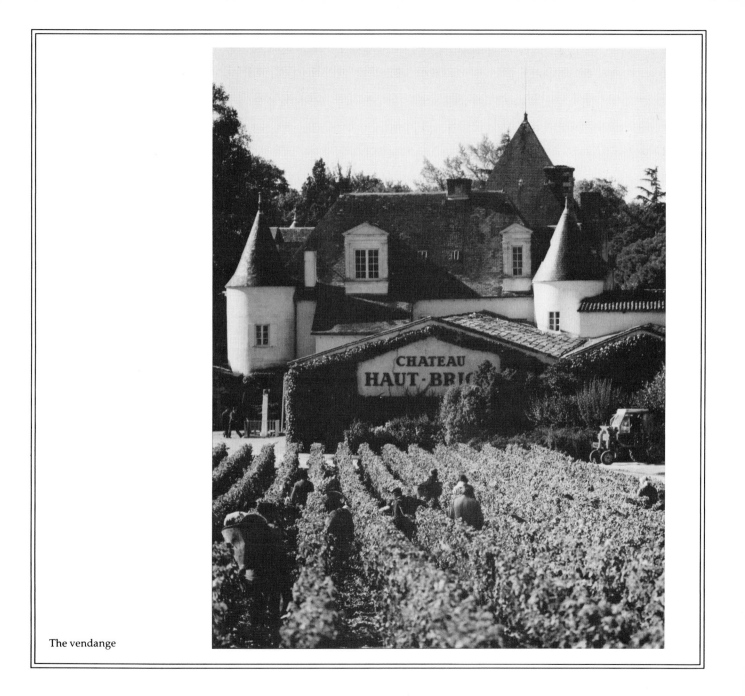

The vendange

Locke also wrote in his *Journal*:

'The best wine at Bordeaux, which is that of Médoc or Pontac – this was worth 80 or 100 crowns. For this the English may thank their own folly for, whereas some years since the same wine was sold for 50 or 60 crowns per tun, the fashionable sending over orders to have the best wine sent them at any rate they have, by striveing who should get it, brought it up to that price. But very good wines may be had here for 35, 40 & 50 crowns per tun.'

Then on 13 July 1683 John Evelyn, the diarist, wrote:

'I had this day much discourse with Monsieur Pontaque, son of the wise Prime President of *Bourdeaux*. This gent, was owner of that excellent *Vignoble* of Pontaque & Obrien, whence the choicest of our *Burdeaux* wines come and I think I may truly say of him . . . . that much learning had made him madd . . . . For the rest he spake all languages, was very rich, an handsome person & well-bred: aged about 45'.

This was François-Auguste. That Haut-Brion was often called Pontac seems likely from a further note in Locke's *Journal*, dated 20 September 1678.

'. . . between 40 & 50 (crowns), which was the price of the best sort of Graves Wine, except Pontac which was sold for 80 or 100, and some others of a peculiar note'. The 'Graves Wine' was almost certainly red, for there is no evidence that the white Graves was regarded as of any great distinction in England, although there was a demand for the sweet wine. (A sale of 105 hogsheads of strong fine Priniac [Preignac] and Bomas [Bommes] French Prize Wines and Stum [unfermented or partly fermented grape juice] was advertised in the *London Gazette* in June 1706.)

Early imports

Ironically enough, it would appear that the Anglo-French warfare at the beginning of the 18th century had a stimulating effect on the imports of Bordeaux and other wines if not exactly as planned. For from about 1703 onwards a regular arrival in London, and occasionally in Southampton and Plymouth, of captured prizes was announced by the Principal Commissioners for Prizes in issue after issue of the twice-weekly official *London Gazette*. Part at least of these wines were sold, customs duties paid, in City of London coffee houses such as Lloyd's in Lombard Street (the precursor of Lloyd's today) and the Marina in Birchin Lane. Although Cyril Ray in his *Lafite* (1978) gives the first advertisements there to the later-established first-growth as being in (May) 1707 to 'Lafit, Margouze and La Tour', two years earlier, in May 1705, an advertisement appeared stating that 'On Thursday the 24th Instant will be exposed to sale at Three in the Afternoon precisely, 200 Hogsheads of Neat

Choice New Red Obrian and Pontack Prize-Wines (just landed). Two Hogsheads in a lot'. A fortnight later 230 hogsheads of 'new Pontac and Margoos wines' were announced, and in June 1706 were sold '60 Hogsheads and 4 Tierces of French new Pontack and Margoos Claret, lying in a Vault in Mincing-Lane'.

Finally, to complete the record of these early imports of Haut-Brion, a few days after the sale in May 1707 that included the other three later first growths, was 'exposed to Sale at Lloyd's Coffee-house in Lombard Street at two in the Afternoon precisely, 200 Hogsheads of new French Obrian Clarets, taken and condemned as Prize out of the Ship Liberty, lying at Wiggin's Key'.

In view of the fact that Locke stated about 30 years earlier that Pontac endeavoured to produce 50 tuns (= 200 *barriques*/hogsheads) every year, the quantities recorded as seized and for sale seem extraordinarily large. Moreover, a few days afterwards 400 hogsheads and ten tierces 'of extraordinary new French claret' were advertised to be followed at the end of June by '172 Hogsheads of French Prize Clarets in 86 lots at 15 1. per Hogshead'. This would work out at £1.00 a dozen.

Presumably Monsieur de Pontac had been paid for his wine before it left Bordeaux, but someone must have lost out along the way, and for where had it been destined if not England?

Division of the estate François-Auguste de Pontac died childless in 1694, and the estate was divided between a sister, Thérèse d'Aulède de Lestonnac, who was married to Jean-Denis d'Aulède, owner of Château Margaux, and a nephew, Louis-Arnaud Leconte, Captal de la Tresne. It was divided in the proportion of two-thirds and one-third respectively. Madame d'Aulède's daughter Catherine, married Count François-Joseph de Fumel. Their son, Louis, inherited the two properties of Margaux and Haut Brion in 1747, a couple of years before his death in 1749. His son, Joseph de Fumel, then inherited. Not only was he proprietor of Margaux, but also Baron de Pauillac. The two properties were separated in 1768 when his daughter married the Comte d'Hargicourt of Margaux. But already in 1749 Haut-Brion had been split up, presumably owing to the holding of the Tresne family, and in 1770 the division became clearer, with the smaller portion, without the *château*, passing to the Marquis de la Tresne, and being known as the Chai-Neuf. It was to remain separated until 1840.

An interesting piece of information from these times, reported in account books preserved at the *château*, was that the *maître de chai* bottled 13 *barriques* of the 1764 vintage in January 1769, and then bottled a further quantity nine years later – 13 years in cask! Not only were binnable bottles then very much in their early days, but *château*-bottling was very uncommon for other than the use of the owners and was usually regarded with disfavour by the *régisseur*, whose main aim was to get rid of the wine as soon as possible, in order to avoid the labour and the loss of wine through the ullage and the racking.

Thomas Jefferson

Another distinguished foreign visitor to Haut-Brion was Thomas Jefferson, in the course of a tour through southern France in 1787. Among the '4 vineyards of first quality' he lists 'Hautbrion, belonging ⅔ to M.Comte de Femelle [Fumel], who has engaged to Barton a merchant, the other ⅓ to the Comte de Toulouse. The whole is 75 *tonneaux*.' The American envoy failed to buy a *barrique* of the 1784 vintage from the Comte de Fumel, who only had four left. 'I offered him 600 pounds for one of his barriques but he refused. I ought to get two cases [50 bottles per case was then normal] from the first hogshead he draws off. It is very much exaggerated to pay three pounds a bottle for a wine bought directly from the Estate, but this vintage has such a reputation that those who have it are getting these prices.' (This sounds like the demand today for Pétrus!). Apparently the 'opening price' for the distinguished 1784 was £325.00 a *barrique* (300 bottles), and by 1789 was worth £700.00.

In the 18th century, up to the Revolution, very large profits were made by the later-designated first-growths. Haut-Brion appears to have been less profitable than Lafite and Latour, where, in the middle of the century, the production costs were no more than one-third of the revenues, giving an average net profit of 495 *livres* a *tonneau*. Haut-Brion's average profit per *tonneau* was estimated at 257 *livres*.

Subsequent owners

The Comte Joseph de Fumel was an important figure in Bordeaux; in 1773 he was made governor of the Château Trompette, the seat of the local *parlement*, and later became governor of Guyenne. He also greatly improved the property of Haut-Brion, laying out a garden and a park, of which the latter is still partly extant. In the early days of the Revolution he had his plate melted down to help the poor of Bordeaux and Pessac, and in March 1790, aged 73, he was made mayor of Bordeaux. However, four years later, when the Revolution was at its height, he was arrested and guillotined, following his daughter who had been executed a few days earlier. This seems to have been a somewhat unusual case, for generally the very rich proprietors were only accused and sentenced if in some way they had opposed the regime, emigrated or helped a relative to escape – as happened with Lafite and Latour. Fumel's niece and nephew, Pons and

The south front

Laure, both spent seven or eight months in prison, but soon after their release the property was restored to them. However they only kept it a few years, sold it to someone whose identity is not at present known. While Pons went abroad and appears not to have been heard of since, Laure Fumel was briefly married to Count Hector Brane, who had to flee abroad but was later to be distinguished as the owner of Brane-Mouton, and afterwards Brane-Cantenac. The complications that followed over Château Margaux did not affect the disposed-of Haut-Brion, but can be followed in Nicholas Faith's *Château Margaux* (Christie's Wine Publications, 1980). Then in 1801 that agile but able politician, Talleyrand, bought Haut-Brion for 255,000 francs. How much time and attention Talleyrand devoted to Haut-Brion is unknown, but now being foreign minister, he sold it after four years to a banker, Michel, for 300,000 francs. Twenty years later it was sold to Monsieur Beyerman, the well-known merchant, and to Monsieur Comyns, a stockbroker, this time for 525,000 francs. The pair quarrelled about the proceeds, a lawsuit ensued and in March 1836 it was again put up for sale. The sale notice can be seen today in the *château*. Valued at 250,000 francs, it fell to Monsieur Eugène Larrieu for 277,000 francs. The area, which included the *château* but only two-thirds of the whole estate, was given as 91 hectares, with 40 to 50 under vines. In 1840 M.Larrieu managed to buy the separated part for 60,000 francs, and ever since it has remained as one vineyard, albeit divided by the Bordeaux-Arcachon main road. M.Larrieu's son, Amadée, who became a *député* and, in 1870, the *préfet* of the *département*, took a considerable interest in the estate and modernised the *chais*. He died in 1873, and was succeeded by his son, Eugène, who lived only until 1896, and was succeeded by nephews who, as not infrequently happens in France under the Napoleonic laws of inheritance, did not get on well together. The property was mortgaged to the Compagnie Algérienne, a banking concern, which foreclosed on them in 1920. The bank sold off part of the property adjoining the vineyard for building, a step that must since have caused a good deal of heart-rending within the estate. The whole property seems to have passed through more than one owner, including the Société des Glacières de Paris, who in 1922 handed it over, as his share of the assets, to M.André Gibert, a banker, on his retirement. M.Gibert does not seem to have been particularly interested in his property, and during his occupation the wines did not pass through a very distinguished period. In 1934 Monsieur Gibert offered it to the city of Bordeaux on the condition that they maintained the vineyard 'in perpetuity'. The corporation, which in past years had already suffered some embarrassment with Château Kirwan, declined, and in the following year it was bought in by Mr Clarence Dillon, the American banker for

2,350,000 francs – after he had been offered Château Margaux and Cheval-Blanc, also up for sale in those difficult times. At that time the estate ran to 48 hectares, of which 36 were under vines. Today it is 53 hectares, 45.5 being under vines.

Variations in quality

Returning to the wine, it would appear that from about the time of the French Revolution Haut-Brion suffered something of an eclipse. In Wilhelm Franck's classic survey of Bordeaux wines, published first in 1824, he wrote, 'for several years it has lost its reputation because too much manure is used. It cannot be put in bottle until six or seven years after the harvest, although other first growths are drinkable at the end of five years'. Moreover, to judge from the evidence of Christie's catalogues it had not much appeal in England, the vital market for the first growths. Whereas the three Médocs from time to time appeared for sale from the 1780s onwards, the first reference to Haut-Brion that I have been able to find was in 1839, when some non-vintage, described in the auctioneer's note as 'light Bordeaux', was sold; and the first vintage wine shown was the sale of the 1834 – a fine but small vintage – in 1844, when it fetched the very good price of 80s. a dozen, as was also given then for Lafite 1834.

It seems not unlikely that this was not a very good time in general for the Graves estates in the vicinity of Bordeaux. For although in the 1855 classification Haut-Brion, with its historic background, could scarcely be omitted in a list nominally of all Bordeaux and not just the Médoc, why not La Mission-Haut-Brion and Pape Clément?

It is said, however, that Haut-Brion improved after the reunification of its estate, and certainly it was outstanding in the difficult post-phylloxera years of the last century. (Though it is difficult to believe entirely the claim made in a brochure issued by the *château* that the vineyard was reconstituted with American-grafted vines by 1900. If so they would have been very young, while most of the other classed growths took many more years to achieve a complete changeover.) For in most years from 1889 to 1899 Haut-Brion fetched a higher price than any of the other first growths, with an exceptional one for the times of 5,200 francs for the excellent 1890, compared with a top figure of 4,000 francs for the other firsts. It also had a special *réclame* for its 1899 and 1900, topping the list for the former at 2,600 francs: 200 more than for Lafite.

The twentieth century

Like the other firsts, and indeed a great number of the *crus classés*, it was under fixed-price contract for a period of years from 1906 onwards, but by 1918 it was free and this vintage was bought early in 1918 for 5,500 francs by the Bordeaux firm of Eschenauer, (compared with 1,650 francs for Lafite and Château

Margaux under contract, and 2,650 for Latour). But a greater sensation was caused on the Bordeaux market when Haut-Brion's 1918 vintage was sold for 8,000 francs a *tonneau*. The other leaders were again contracted at about 2,650 francs.

In spite of a series of wonderful vintages, the 1920s were difficult times for Bordeaux, if a great deal less so than the succeeding decade. No doubt Monsieur Gibert found his 12-year ownership difficult, and as a result sold off some of the adjacent land for building. It does not seem that he made much impact on the wine making. Frequent changes of ownership are likely to reflect badly on an estate's wines, and I am inclined to believe that the first 40 years of the present century were not a particularly successful period for Haut-Brion. However, over the years few bottles of these vintages have come my way. Many years ago I remember a magnum of 1906 with pleasure, and, curiously enough, it was at Mouton-Rothschild in 1966 that I was surprised by the excellent condition still of the 1908, which had a slight burnt taste and by the 1914 – both poor vintages – which had some decay but still retained a fine flavour.

I drank the fine 1920 once or twice when it was around 25–30 years old, but I thought the 1928 and 1929 very disappointing, a view confirmed at a pre-sale tasting at Christie's in 1979 of a range of Haut-Brion vintages, in which both wines had a heavy, porty, cooked flavour. Was one or other of them pasteurised, as the 1928 Lafite was? But at the same tasting the 1926 was very distinguished, though the 1924 was past it: but that was no condemnation of a 55-year-old claret. And I remember a splendid 1921 drunk in Bordeaux in 1973 at Cruses' table. With a big colour, rich nose and complete flavour, it had probably benefited from never having been moved.

In 1972 Joseph Berkmann gave a dinner in London of 13 vintages of Haut-Brion, from 1906 to 1962. Although it did not last, the 1922 – a huge, indifferent vintage – was perhaps the most interesting wine of the evening, as it was surprisingly fruity and held 'all the way'.

The present owners I have no recollection of the Haut-Brions of the 30s, but it is clear that a change began after the war, with the very fine 1945. By then Georges Delmas was the *régisseur*, and Clarence Dillon's nephew, Seymour Weller, who took French citizenship, directed the property until his death only a few years ago. In 1953 Clarence Dillon's son, Douglas, became American ambassador to France, and later joined President Eisenhower's and then President Kennedy's administrations. His daughter Joan, who had married Prince Charles of Luxembourg, assumed the estate's administration with her husband, and when

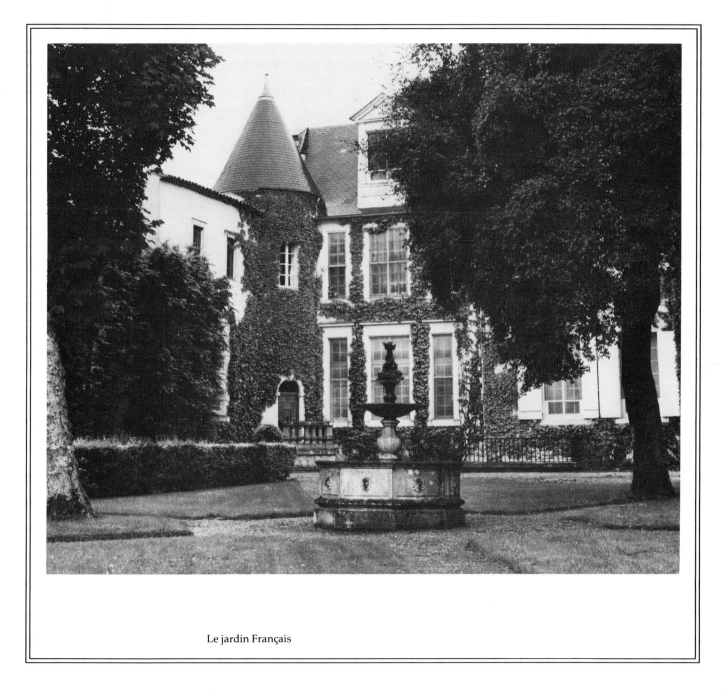

Le jardin Français

the latter died in 1977, she married the Duc de Mouchy, member of a very old French family, one of whose ancestors had been governor of Guyenne in the 18th century. They now run Haut-Brion as director-general and president respectively. In 1961 Georges Delmas passed over the *régisseur*-ship to his son Jean, one of the most experienced and esteemed *régisseurs* in Bordeaux. Since then I believe that the standard and reputation of Haut-Brion wines have risen. In 1960 the estate had startled Bordeaux by the installation of a battery of electronically-controlled stainless steel vats. Four years later they were followed in 1964 by the new owners of Latour. More recently some fine new, stone-pillared cellars were dug in 1973, and in 1977 a collection of clones from its three grape varieties, *cabernet sauvignon*, *cabernet franc* and *merlot*, were planted in an experiment to produce clones that would in time evolve in vines to result in higher quality, greater quantity and better resistance to disease.

Haut-Brion today

In the 42 hectares planted in black grapes, 55 per cent is *cabernet sauvignon*, 20 per cent *cabernet franc* and 25 per cent *merlot*. The 3½ hectares of white grapes are planted 50–50 *sémillon* and *sauvignon*. Average production is 120–130 *tonneaux*, though more than this in the record 1982 vintage. A second wine, Bahans-Haut-Brion, is produced from 20–30 *tonneaux* of the total output. The sale used largely to be confined to French restaurants, but now it may occasionally be seen in Britain and in the USA. Although a sound wine I have not found it to have the interest or quality of Latour's second wine, Les Forts de Latour. However, greatly in demand is the *château*'s dry white wine, Haut-Brion Blanc, of which only about eight to ten *tonneaux* are produced, and sold at a price comparable with that of the red wine. It is made from equal proportions of *sauvignon* and *sémillon*. The Duc de Mouchy told me that his most difficult job was refusing orders for the Haut-Brion Blanc; 1,000 dozen bottles do not go very far.

Compared with the fruity, well-rounded but often elegant Médocs on the one hand, and the soft, easy-to-drink St.-Emilions and Pomerols on the other, the small body of fine red Graves have not always found it easy to establish their worth. For they are different. They have an earthy 'bricky' bouquet and flavour; and they are drier than the leading classed growths of the other districts, lacking the voluptuousness and fullness of a leading Médoc, the richness of a great St.-Emilion or Pomerol.

What most of them do have, and Haut-Brion in particular, is a finesse and refinement, along with an aroma that often rises more readily from the glass than with many other leading clarets. Their colour in their early years is seldom as deep as in, say, the Pauillacs and St.-Estèphes, and they tend to develop earlier, and perhaps are generally less long lived than such wines. Somewhat different, 'earthier' than the others, is the neighbouring La Mission-Haut-Brion: big in colour and nose, backward in development. Every now and again the two are set against each other, but this seems to me mistaken, as are, say, comparisons between Lafite and Latour. They are different styles of wine, arising mostly from the soil, partly from the *cépage* (La Mission-Haut-Brion has ten per cent more *cabernet sauvignon*). If it is 'size', combined with strength that one is looking for, one might choose La Mission, but for finesse then Haut-Brion surely has the palm. It is a tradition in Bordeaux that fine clarets should not be opened, or at least seriously appraised, until they are ten years old. Accordingly, from time to time I have arranged dinners at which the ten-year-old first growths have been drunk. It is difficult to know where in the tastings to place Haut-Brion. Usually it comes after the 'lighter' Médocs, such as Margaux and Lafite, and before the 'heavy' Mouton-Rothschild and Latour; and before the right-bank firsts. On occasion Haut-Brion has come top, as the most advanced and well-balanced, but always it has shown comparatively well, and held beautifully in the glass. Classic claret!

Salle des gardes – now the tasting room

Burgundy then and now
Anthony Hanson, MW

Burgundy's great reputation was made by fast-maturing light red wines. Only since the 19th century has popular demand been for deeper coloured wines with greater body. The fashion has lasted 150 years, but, in the context of a reputation which goes back 1,500 years, may still be temporary. And if our expectations of fine red burgundy were slightly different, perhaps we would more often be delighted with it.

If one compares the writings of Burgundian and English wine writers it is clear that only in the last century did long vatting times become commonplace. Here is A. C. Henderson, in the *History of Ancient and Modern Wines* (London, 1824): 'Wines such as Pommard or Volnay are allowed to remain in the vat only for twenty to thirty hours . . . these wines are accordingly fit for drinking in the second or third year after the vintage.'

Dr Lavalle states[1] that the principal points of wine making in Burgundy have been the same in every epoch from the sixth to his own century: bring together the grapes in vats, let them ferment there a certain time, squash them, then press them. Removing the stalks was never suggested, and the juice was never left in contact with the skins and stalks for more than a few days. He went on to

[1]*Histoire et Statistique de la Vigne et des Grands Vins de la Côte d'Or* (1855).

admit, however, that personal taste and the fashion of his time had varied the details. At the expense of finesse and bouquet all the *pinot blanc* and *pinot beurrot* were being pulled up in the vineyards (where for centuries they had been planted amongst *pinots noirs*), to obtain wines of deeper colour and more firmness.

In Cyrus Redding's third edition of *A History and Description of Modern Wines* (1851), the manner of making the best wines of the Côte d'Or is described: 'The grapes are commonly trodden before they are thrown into the vat; a part of the stalks are then taken out and the must is suffered to ferment. The fermentation . . . lasts from thirty to forty-eight hours, if the weather is hot, and from three to eight days, and even twelve days, if it be cold. . . .'

The longer vatting did not relate to a wine maker's desire to extract colour through maceration. Quite simply, vat houses were constructed with little care. As Dr Lavalle describes, there was often no roof, and the doors were ill-fitting – it was a matter of good luck if the temperature inside the vat house rose above that outside, so it might take a week or more for fermentation to begin.

Cyrus Redding states that from the second year in bottle, the fullest bodied and hardiest wines had attained their highest degree of perfection – all that could be desired thereafter was that they should not deteriorate.

One should perhaps be wary of treating him as an authority on 19th-century burgundy – he contradicts himself in different parts of his book, places Chambolle-Musigny on the Côte de Beaune, Vosne and Morey on the Chalonnaise, and even rates white Hermitage more highly than Montrachet! But his facts seem to have been gathered at first hand. There is nothing comparable to Mr Henderson's charming admission: 'The description of the mode of conducting the fermentation of the grapes in Burgundy is partly copied from notes made on the spot, in the autumn of 1822: but as I unfortunately did not arrive there in time to witness the vintage, my information is less satisfactory than I could wish, and possibly, in some respects, erroneous.'

Henry Vizetelly's assessments of Burgundy[2] date from his service as wine juror for Great Britain at the Vienna exhibition of 1873. Even moderate age wore out the best burgundies, he says, as was shown by several of the samples. He rated an 1869 Richebourg at four years old 'far superior to the more ancient vintages'.

It is French writers who give us the best insight into what burgundies of the past were really like. Here is A. Jullien in his *Topographie de Tous les Vignobles*

[2]*The Wines of the World, Characterized and Classed* (London, 1875).

Connus (Paris, 1816): 'Since the Revolution the amount of land planted with vines has considerably increased, several proprietors having converted low and marshy land to vineyards. Some have introduced fertilisers or brought new soil to the hillsides, in order to obtain larger harvests, others have replaced old vines with young or even substituted common vine-types for the fine varieties. People who buy the products of these degenerated vineyards, or who have had poor vintage wine passed off to them as from a good year, think that the wines of Burgundy are not what they were in the past. But . . . if Burgundy produces more common wines than was the case thirty years ago, the number of good growths, far from diminishing, has spread by several hillsides' worth'. For A. Jullien, red burgundy from the Côte d'Or of a good year united in just proportions all the qualities which constituted perfect wines . . . a beautiful colour, much perfume and a delicious taste. At the same time they were full-bodied, fine, delicate and racy, without being too heady.

They had a bouquet which was their own, and which often only developed after three or four years. He went on to state that wines from Volnay, Pommard and Beaune could be drunk from the second year after their harvest (being agreeable and very frank), whereas wines from Nuits should be left till their third, or even fourth year – and travelled admirably over land and sea to boot.

One of the main reasons why burgundies were drinkable young was the presence of white grapes mingled with the red. Camille Rodier records (*Le Clos de Vougeot*, Dijon, 1949) that in the mid-19th century two-fifths of the famous Clos was planted with *pinot blanc*. The delicate wine which resulted had a distinct partridge-eye tint.

Wine making on the Côte de Beaune was first described in detail by the Abbé Tainturier in 1763. On the first day the *vigneron* would fill his vat with grapes, on the second he would climb naked into it, piercing with difficulty to the bottom of the vat and going back and forth. 'Soon the broken grape gives out its juice, he can move more freely, the squashing is less impeded – an hour or two of this exercise is needed for a vat of 20 to 25 hogsheads. After three or four hours, if the juice is of fine red colour, with a lively and penetrating aroma, it is time to draw off the vat.' A different technique was used on the Côte de Nuits, where the juice and grapes were not drawn off for pressing until after the fermentation had been completed. Vatting times on both Côtes depended to a large extent on the ambient temperature, varying, according to Dr Morelot in 1819, from thirty hours to eight or ten days if it took that long for the fermentation to begin.

The main innovations in wine making technique (which resulted in deeper coloured burgundies being produced in the the 19th century than at any time previously) can be found in the instructions issued by Chaptal (who was Napoleon's minister of agriculture), published in 1801. The harvest could be improved by the addition of sugar; squashing of the grapes could be done by means of a 'long-handled plane'; one or two cauldrons of boiling must could be added to the vat, and the floating hat of grape skins could be kept beneath the surface by means of a close-fitting cover. This produced a style of wine which foreigners particularly appreciated, and wines which were sturdy enough to travel well. The arrival of the railways must have made easier the transport of Rhône or Midi wines used for 'improving'; and brandy was beginning to be added to wines destined for export markets.

Writing on Côte d'Or vinification in 1864, A. de Vergnette-Lamotte declared that 'We have had to conform to the taste of the drinkers . . . by using large wine tuns we can obtain up to twenty days vatting, and deliver for consumption wines which are rich in extracted matter and above all heavily charged with tannins'. There was of course very little legislation or control to protect the consumer from substitution or fraud. Dr Lavalle encountered a *négociant* based outside Burgundy and asked him how he had managed to amass enormous profits in so few years, to be told: 'It is by always selling Burgundy without either harvesting or buying any.'

No doubt the style of wine he was blending was the deep coloured, full flavoured wine which the 19th century liked – a far cry from the partridge-eye tinted wine from the vermilion *pinot* which was transported to Rheims to celebrate the coronation of Charles IV in 1321 or that of Philippe VI in 1328. Late 20th-century burgundy seems a compromise between the two styles.

One thing about Beaune wine has never changed however: it has always been expensive. In a royal enactment of 1337, setting the tax on wines distributed in Paris, Beaune wine was given the highest rate, at five *sous*, where Gascony rated four *sous*, Auxerre two *sous* and local wine from the Ile de France 1 1/3 *sous*. Today there is no prospect of it ever selling at anything but a luxury price. For how to buy it one cannot do better than follow Dr Lavalle's advice of 1855: 'Be very strict over quality, be very easy over price.'

Favourite wine lists
David Peppercorn, MW

When I began to consider why it is that I immediately thought of some wine lists
as favourites above others, I realised that these were the wine lists which had
made decisive contributions towards my enjoyment of a particular occasion.
Eating in restaurants should indeed be occasions for enjoyment, and the
satisfaction we finally experience is a skilfully blended amalgam of food, wine,
service and that most elusive quality which is somehow best expressed in the
French word 'ambience', hard to define, but so easy to recognise when it is
absent.

   Clearly there are people who go to restaurants only to eat; there can be far
fewer who go solely to drink, but most of us enjoy the totality of the experience.
In this sense, it is to the genius of the *patron* and the restaurant as an expression
of his personality that we respond. When his priorities correspond to ours, and
when he succeeds in giving full expression to his dreams, then we experience
something worth remembering, and something we wish to return to.

   Most of us, at one time or another, have been faced with the wine list as a
work of reference. Perhaps one day in the not so distant future such lists will
become available on microfilm, to be gravely considered before ever one dares
set foot in the restaurant. For, unless the restaurant forms part of a hotel, which
opens up quite different possibilities, it is difficult to do justice to such a list

and at the same time pay any attention to one's guests, to say nothing of keeping their very natural curiosity at bay. Many serious establishments today offer a list which is combined with the menu, an excellent formula since both may be considered in concert, as they should be, and other interested parties can also get in on the act. It also banishes once and for all the problem of the 'missing wine list' and saves both time and frayed nerves.

The Four Seasons

It may seem unduly quixotic if I begin my quest in the New World. Certainly, when I first crossed the Atlantic, it was not in the expectation of any memorable gastronomic experiences. All the reports I had heard from those friends whose judgement I trusted suggested, on the contrary, a gastronomic desert, where if one could abstain from junk food, the pounds would soon be falling away through sheer lack of temptation. By the greatest good luck and the kindness of Gerald Asher, one of the first things I did in New York was to attend the California Barrel Tasting at The Four Seasons. This introduced me to two remarkable Middle Europeans, Hungarian Paul Kovi and Transylvanian Tom Margittai, who have created at The Four Seasons what is, for me, the one authentically great restaurant in the States, as this term would be understood in Europe.

The United States boasts a number of restaurants, invariably very expensive, which aim to reproduce a French restaurant in an American setting. For anyone used to the real thing, they are, in the main, pale imitations, far removed from the originals. It is very noticeable that when French chefs and waiters are transplanted from their home ground, with its bracingly critical clientele, into less exacting and knowledgeable terrain, they frequently acquire an ostentation coupled with that especially Gallic brand of lofty condescension that does not augur well for either our digestion or our bank balance. It is the achievement of Kovi and Margittai that they have created at The Four Seasons something which is inimitably American and truly original.

It would require someone far better qualified than I to do justice to the refined invention of The Four Seasons' kitchen, where the Swiss chef, Seppi Rengli, uses *nouvelle cuisine* concepts to weave a myriad of gossamer variations to titillate even the most jaded palates. I especially remember the delight of watching some American friends thoroughly enjoying mouth-watering calves' brains ingeniously incorporated into a salad, in the certain knowledge that they would never have ordered them, let alone eaten them, had they had an inkling of what they were! The use of the best fresh produce, with seafood and vegetables playing a leading role, is at the heart of The Four Seasons' formula. Dishes such

The inimitably American and truly original Four Seasons

as Filet of Boston Sole with Sea Urchin Butter, Quail and Lobster Ragoût and Cabbage Stuffed with Pheasant, all from this winter's luncheon menu, give some idea of the flavour of the place.

One of my first and most lasting impressions of this restaurant is of its setting; quite simply, it has one of the most beautiful rooms conceivable, with tables arranged around a square pond. The service is unobtrusive and completely professional. Everything is ordained to give a sense of relaxed well-being. The menu appears on a stiffish parchment paper which then opens up to reveal the wine list covering two facing sides. So ordering is made as simple as possible. Paul Kovi tells me that this concept has helped create wine discussion round the table and has been appreciated by their clientele.

He and Tom Margittai are justly proud of being pioneers of Californian wines. By 1968, they had a selection of 40–50 Californian wines which was unheard of anywhere in the United States, including California itself, at that time. Today, some 25 per cent of the list is devoted to Californian wines and 45 per cent are from France. But Germany and Italy, as well as Hungary, Spain, Austria and Switzerland, are also represented.

This is certainly the place to explore the wines of California. Interestingly enough, the selection of American wines – for there are also examples from Washington State, Hammondsport and Hudson Valley – are arranged according to district and not by grape variety. Not only will you find the classics here from Heitz, Mondavi, Ridge, Phelps, Trefethen and St.-Jean, but many others, encompassing both fine examples made by the large companies, such as Paul Masson, and small, lesser-known wineries unearthed by Paul Kovi.

Among the French wines, pride of place, not unnaturally, goes to Bordeaux. Paul Kovi reports that they have been buying Bordeaux 'futures' since the early 1960s, and their selection reflects this. So, today, one can enjoy the very drinkable 1976s at fair prices or, for special occasions, there is everything from Lafite 1945 or 1949, through the less obvious but superb Ausone 1962 and Haut-Brion 1967, to almost modestly priced Gruaud-Larose 1967 or 1970. The burgundies show some good domains, but it is easier to find mature whites than reds, a situation all too familiar in France as well. Outside France, the Italian wines show the most imagination, with wines like the Spanna Campi Raudii of Vallana and Lungarotti's Cabernet Sauvignon. Like other restaurateurs I spoke to, Paul Kovi confirmed that not all is revealed on the wine list; they have a further 90 to 100 wines in smaller quantities which are offered for private parties or as special suggestions from time to time.

If The Four Seasons is something unique, there is another sort of American restaurant which deserves to be searched out and patronised. This is the type which aims to serve the finest quality produce in a simple, unadorned state. Two such restaurants have given me much pleasure, Anthony's at Pier 4 in Boston, and Sparks Steak House on East 46 Street, New York. Both reflect the special personalities of their energetic owners.

Pier 4

Anthony Athanas is a remarkable man of Albanian origin. Small and dapper, quiet yet restlessly observant, he has created at Pier 4, with its marvellous panorama of Boston harbour, a restaurant that is quintessentially American. The first thing that struck me was the sheer size of the place. Hundreds of people can sit down to eat at the same time, and with the enormous range of meal times which are accepted here, some will be arriving for an early dinner, while others are finishing a late lunch. There is no booking, yet you never have long to wait for a table. There are many such places in America in terms of size, mostly serving food which is banal and lacklustre. But Anthony Athanas proves that superb organisation can provide delicious, straightforward food with friendly, efficient service. This is a place to enjoy the best of the east coast seafood, especially its oysters, clams (much more succulent than the European sort) and, above all, the incomparable lobsters.

Peter Holt, originally from England, is in overall charge of the wine list under Anthony Athanas's personal supervision. Mr Athanas is another pioneer as far as Californian wines are concerned. The list, in traditional format, begins with an impressive sweep of 39 Chardonnays, providing halves and magnums in a number of instances. There is a selection of Late Harvest wines conveniently in half-bottles. But if you thought that the Old World had been banished to second place, a formidable list of over 40 white burgundies follows, with an unusual white St Aubin moving to the rarefied heights of the Musigny Blanc and Leflaive's Bienvenues-Bâtard. White bordeaux are unusually comprehensive, with Carbonnieux and Malartic, as well as Domaine de Chevalier, Laville and that great rarity, Haut-Brion Blanc. There are some very well selected Sauternes, including Yquem '67 and Suduiraut '59. Germany is represented by some fine mosels, with Dr Thanisch, Egon Müller, von Schubert, J. J. Prüm and the Bischöfliche Weingüt all represented. The white selection concludes with some memorable Beeren- and Trockenbeerenauslesen, mostly in halves.

Although the opportunities for drinking red wines are more limited, the list does not skimp on them. A fine array of Cabernets and Zinfandels leads on to some exceptional clarets, mostly of the 1970s, but including La Mission 1961 and 1962, Gruaud-Larose 1962 and Trotanoy 1966 and 1967. The red burgundies are

The relaxed elegance of
Taillevant

Anthony Athanas, creator of
Pier 4

briefer, but interesting, with a 1972 Nuits from Gouges and wines from Mérode and the Domaine de la Pousse d'Or. To round off, there are some interesting Italian wines and even some vintage port. By this time it has become clear that Anthony is as passionate about his wines as about everything else that he does. There is a policy of laying down, which is clearly reflected in the range and maturity of wines offered.

Sparks Steakhouse

At Sparks, Pat Cetta and his brother, Michael, run a steak house of more normal proportions, admirably suited to New Yorkers' needs. They grew up in the family butchery business, so this is a place where they understand properly hung meat. They also specialise in lobsters cooked to order and other fresh fish. But, open up the short, simple menu and you find that the Cetta brothers also have a passion for wine.

It takes only a few words with Pat Cetta to discover a kindred spirit anxious to introduce you to the glories of his cellar for, as he explains, the ample printed list represents only the tip of the iceberg. The Sparks cellar boasts 3–4,000 cases, and the 300 items on the list are backed up by another 4–500 ready to replace them. So, my wife and I shared one of the magnificent lobsters and followed it with a sirloin steak, again halved. Pat agreed that American steaks are ridiculously large, but said that that is what the customer demands. However, the British stomach, and our dislike of waste, were cheerfully accommodated. Such food, excellent and simple, provides a perfect backdrop for exploring the delights of the Sparks cellar.

Here, there are two outstanding themes – Californian wines, of course, but also Italian, the only hint of the Cettas' origins. Comparative rarities, such as the marvellous Cabernet Sauvignons of Mirassou Harvest Selection '74, Ridge Montebello '72, Mondavi and Heitz '68 are still listed here, while the Chardonnays include the Mondavi Reserve '79 and St.-Jean's Robert Young '79. There is a fine selection of Late Harvest wines. The fascination of the Italian list is the array of mature vintages, so seldom seen, even in Italy: Gaja's Barbaresco '61, great Barolo vintages back to '47, Gattinaras, Spannas and even Taurasi of '68. Anywhere else, the claret list would be a talking point, with '71s from Cheval Blanc and La Conseillante, and Talbot from '61 and '49, to say nothing of magnums of Latour '66 and Talbot '45!

European favourites have to start in France, still the touchstone of civilised dining. It is unfortunately true that many of the classic cellars are now no more. Shall we ever see the like again of the old Chapon Fin in Bordeaux? It is not only a question of money, but also of fashion. The market in old wines has been transformed in recent years by the auction houses, but French diners are less inclined than ever to drink old wines at high prices, and this has led to the break-up of many fine old cellars. In consequence, many of the best restaurants in France today sadly lack mature wines. Their selections are often superb in terms of quality, but one does not really want to drink classified growths of '75 or the top 1978 Côte d'Or wines yet. So, I have turned to a classic by any standards – Taillevent.

Taillevent

I first met Jean-Claude Vrinat at one of Gault-Millau's marathon Paris tastings, and he is clearly a man who regards his wines as one of the major pillars of his famous restaurant. It was his father who laid the foundations of the cellar immediately after the war in 1946, advised and encouraged by Raymond Baudoin, the founder of the *Revue du Vin de France,* and a celebrated taster at that time. Jean-Claude began working at Taillevent in 1962, but even before that he often accompanied his father on his numerous visits to the wine-producing regions of France. He says that the principles that his father laid down, and which he has always followed, were to represent all the important vineyards of France, to buy only from the best producers, and to look for the best relationship of quality to price. He reckons he consecrates one third of his time to wine, assisted by his wife, especially visiting suppliers' cellars, and never buys without careful tastings.

The atmosphere of Taillevent is wholly conducive to relaxed dining. In spite of its well-deserved fame, the place is delightfully free from any sort of pretension. Everything is slightly understated in a discreet sort of way, the staff know how to be attentive without being obtrusive and the other diners respond by not demanding a show or allowing their natural enjoyment to overflow on to surrounding tables. If I said that it was rather like a club, that does not imply that there is anything stuffy about it, rather that staff and diners seem to be in harmony with each other. Here, excellence is the norm, as you choose and enjoy the *nouvelle cuisine* dishes, with their many nuances of flavour to delight the palate, and find a choice of wines that offer so many possibilities of drinking classic bottles in peak condition. The wine list here can be seen at a glance, although it takes longer than that to absorb all it has to offer. It is similar in size to The Four Seasons, except that there is no menu on the outside and, of course, no Californian wines! What immediately impresses is the strength in depth. There is no more generally enjoyable mature vintage of top quality at present than the '66 bordeaux, and here you can find no fewer than a dozen examples, from Les Ormes de Pez to Haut-Brion. When it comes to the great '70 vintage, there are 21 examples listed, while the deliciously precocious '76 vintage has 25 examples. What is more, this is not just a list of big names; there are plenty of interesting and usually moderately priced wines, such as Château Roudier, Montagne St.-Emilion, available in the '76, '75, '70 and '61 vintages. And how rewarding it is to find '55s such as Lanessan and the delicious Balestard la Tonnelle. The clarets go back as far as Margaux 1934, and there is a note to say that some older rarities are held, which must be ordered in advance, going back apparently to Lafite 1846. I like the way the 1976 first growths have been included, but not, as yet, the '75s.

The red burgundies are less numerous, but hardly less impressive for their range and deft selection. Most of the best names are here: Tollot-Beaut, Rapet, d'Angerville, Rousseau, Gouges, Dujac, Trapet, Roumier, Gaunoux, de Courcel and de Vogüé. There are some excellent '72s and '71s still listed, and examples available of the '69, '66, '64, '62 and '61 vintages. The same care of selection is evident among the white burgundies, and there are some good white bordeaux, both Graves and Sauternes-Barsac. Of the other French wines, the most surprising are some old Juras, Château-Chalon and Vin Jaune of the 1960s. As an interesting footnote, there is a special separate list of champagnes, including the rare and unusual single vineyard Clos des Goisses from Philipponnat.

From all this you will not be surprised to learn that you may have to book two weeks ahead to get a table at Taillevent. Yet success certainly has not spoiled them – the ultimate tribute, perhaps, to Jean-Claude and his devoted staff.

San Domenico

The story of how Gianluigi Morini created the San Domenico at Imola is so fascinating that it deserves an article of its own. If anybody thinks that there are no great restaurants in Italy, this must be the place to convert them. In 1970 Signor Morini created his dream restaurant in the mediaeval house where he was born. The name was taken from the adjoining Dominican convent. The family were farmers who raised pigs and grew vines. The house was acquired by Signor Morini's grandfather at the beginning of the century, and the family opened a shop on the ground floor to sell charcuterie and wine. So he was brought up in an atmosphere where the production and preparation of food and wine were of the essence.

The twist in the tale is that Morini's father wanted advancement for his son, so put him into the local bank. But, as his natural aptitudes developed, his wife and his father supported him when he finally decided he had to become a restaurateur.

Pat Cetta at Sparks
Steakhouse

The 600-year old cellars of San
Domenico

Gianluigi Morini is a perfectionist who is also a natural host. He wants you to feel as relaxed as you would dining at a friend's house. There are only 20 tables, divided between six rooms, so the scale and intimacy of this mediaeval house have been completely retained. He also believes that it is the total experience that matters, so not only must the food and wine be right, but so must the staff, the glass and china, the napkins and tablecloths and, of course, the décor and lighting. There is even a complete programme of classical music for each day of the week, but so discreet you feel that a small band of musicians must be in an adjoining room.

The originality of this restaurant lies in what Signor Morini calls *la cucina di casa* as distinct from traditional Italian restaurant cooking. This means freshly and individually prepared dishes such as used to be served in the great noble houses of Italy. To achieve this he first had to persuade Nino Bergese, the last of the great private chefs, to pass on his secrets to his own talented Valentino Marcattilii, and then take his advice and send him to Illhaeusern, Troisgros and La Pyramide to learn how great kitchens are organised. The results of this experiment could be as important to Italian cooking as Fernand Point's contribution to French cooking.

Perhaps you should tour the wine cellars here even before you consult the list. Those beneath the house are at least 600 years old, and they are joined on to those of the neighbouring Dominican convent, which are even older. The noble brick-built vaults make one of the most beautiful cellars imaginable; no crouching here – you could inspect these cellars in a top hat! They contain one of the greatest collections of wine in Italy, or anywhere else, for here you will find not only all the Italian classics, but also an array of French wines which would make most French restaurateurs envious. There are 30 different Barolos, and every vintage of Mouton-Rothschild from 1945, with the 1920 and 1921 thrown in for good measure. Here are Lafite, Latour, Margaux and Yquem, should you desire them, or the wines of the Domaine de la Romanée-Conti. Magnums, jeroboams and imperials are available. Signor Morini was not jesting when he said he wanted his guests to dine like kings. In all, this remarkable cellar contains around 1,000 different wines.

My final memory of this gem of a restaurant is of rising from the table with that feeling of well-being that its proprietor seeks to give his guests. Signor Morini's great interest in the theatre and film world ensures that the *mise en scène* of your meal at the San Domenico is unforgettable. The food and the wine combine to give a lasting impression of a rare experience enjoyed.

It seems appropriate that this quest should end at home in England, and in the

Gidleigh Park on the edge of Dartmoor

England of the country house. The development of the country house hotel has been one of the most encouraging trends here in recent years. Houses which are now too large and expensive for most people to maintain as homes can make very intimate hotels, especially if the proprietor can retain the illusion that you are a guest at some relaxing house party.

Gidleigh Park

It is ironic that one of the best of the genre should be owned and run by an American couple from Virginia. Paul and Kay Henderson make a perfect team, Kay being a gifted and dedicated cook, and Paul an unobtrusively welcoming host who happens to have a passion for wine. The remarkable thing is that after only four years in the business, Gidleigh Park won Egon Ronay's 'Wine Cellar of the Year' award for 1981. In the preface to his 1982 list, Paul remarked that he had considered their previous list, with 348 wines on it, too large but that now, after ruthless pruning, the new edition offered 358 wines! There speaks the enthusiast. But the remark I most liked was: 'It's silly to spend much money on wine unless you have a reasonable degree of interest in it.' How wise and how honest.

Gidleigh Park is a comfortable house of 12 bedrooms, superbly sited on the edge of Dartmoor. Its mock-Tudor appearance seems at first sight more suited to the stockbroker belt of the home counties, but the comfort and convenience of the interior, and the views up the valley which all its rooms command, soon make you forget this. The modest size of the house makes for a hospitably intimate atmosphere, skilfully preserved by Paul Henderson. The reception rooms are generous in size, so other guests never seem to get in the way, and there is so much to do in the way of walking and sightseeing in the locality that one is never short of exercise or interest.

In such a setting, the wine list which Paul has amazingly assembled in so short a time makes for admirable reading, and certainly deserves detailed study. The declared policy is 'to offer a selection in depth from the classic European growing areas, and at least some choice from all the areas which produce wines of reasonably good quality. The depth of choice from an area indicates first how much *we* like the wines . . . and second, how much demand there is from clients – in 1981, we served more Léoville-Barton 1966 than all Spanish and Italian red wines combined'. There is a good selection of wines at less than £7.50 a bottle, and another feature is the range of halves available, especially if you realise how hard it is to find quality wines in halves nowadays. The other speciality here, not surprisingly, is Californian wine. Paul says he does not know of another restaurant outside America which offers a better choice: a very safe assertion I should think.

One sad but hardly surprising development is that the 1983 list will see the departure of most of the Bordeaux first growths, and of the Domaine de la Romanée-Conti wines. It is simply that, even at Paul's very modest mark-ups on his expensive wines, people at a country hotel like this do not buy them. And £49.00 for Lafite 1962 or £39.00 for Haut-Brion 1962 could hardly be called extravagant pricing. One hopes that people are still keeping and drinking these great wines at home. It would be tragic if a generation were to grow up in this country which never had the chance of drinking these French masterpieces. Sadder still to think of them going down uncomprehending expense-account throats, or being bought by those who collect 'labels'.

The list is full of useful snippets of information, and of course Paul himself is at hand to give you the benefit of the advice of someone who is both an experienced taster of fine wines and who has tasted all the wines on his list.

I think the strong points are an admirable champagne selection, with some very reasonable prices, the marvellous Californian wines, and some lovely German wines from the best estates, especially the mosels. The clarets deserve special mention. The very young vintages are not listed yet; instead, we get mature wines, such as two lesser 1975s, only two 1970s, but a selection of 1966s, 1964s, 1962s and 1961s. So you can be confident of drinking wines at their best and are spared the exasperation of seeing lines of marvellous wines which are not yet drinkable. The burgundy selection is limited, but very well chosen from good *domaines* and *négociants*. There are also some very good Rhônes. The one weak spot is white burgundy, and this is something Paul is already seeking to improve. It is not that there are not some good wines, but the choice is very limited.

It would be a serious injustice to Kay Henderson not to mention the food. She has developed a range of dishes of great delicacy and refinement, marked by real inventiveness, so that one looks forward to one's dinner with anticipation. The food here provides a perfect foil to this marvellous list of wines, and one can then be assured of a sound night's sleep afterwards, the ultimate test of a well-balanced meal.

I hope these thoughts may either introduce you to fresh delights or revive pleasant memories. They certainly show that there are many types of wine list worthy of admiration, all of which reflect the individuality and flair of their dedicated creators. Writing this has awakened in me a powerful nostalgia and a determination to return to these great cellars, preferably before you have the chance of drinking them dry!

Brunello di Montalcino
Burton Anderson

Most other wines of such lofty status took decades, even centuries, to establish their niches in the hierarchy. But Brunello di Montalcino arrived so suddenly – a decade ago who outside Italy had heard of, let alone tried, this luxury red? – that it looms as one of the wine world's modern wonders.

Cinderella story? Not exactly. Brunello's instant majesty is rather more the fable of an aristocratic Tuscan sensing that the moment was right to emerge from the cellar and join the jet set. The tale would not be complete without a measure of mystery which, as I think about it, seems to be the secret of Brunello's success.

The origins

The wine's history spans a scant 113 years to when Ferruccio Biondi-Santi isolated the Brunello clone of *sangiovese* in the vineyards of his Greppo estate at Montalcino, the fortress town 25 miles south of Siena where, in the mid-16th century, the Sienese Republic made its last, bitter stand against the Florentines. Biondi-Santi wines from the pre-phylloxera vintages of 1888 and 1891 have held remarkably well, to the awe of the privileged few who have tasted them. The four bottles of 1888 are no longer for sale at the cellars, but the 21 bottles of 1891 are, at 6,000,000 lire (about £2,700) each.

My first taste of Brunello, in May 1971, prompted the note: 'At last, a Tuscan *grand cru!'* That 1964 *riserva* from Biondi-Santi, though youthful, left no doubt about its *noblesse oblige*. Its authority in colour, bouquet, weight, texture and length on the palate came as a revelation. With its intriguing dark label, already handsome price (3,000 lire then, 240,000 lire now[1]) and tales of immortality to enhance the legend, Brunello commanded more attention than my dozen or so trustworthy chiantis of the time.

Biondi-Santi

Since then, Biondi-Santi Brunello has surfaced abroad like a phantom in black from chianti country, mystifying merchants who had been led to believe that such prices were reserved for the likes of Pétrus and Lafite. Those figures sum up one of the most brilliant sales coups in the annals of wine. No ads, no gimmicks, no famous-artist labels or famous-author books; owner Franco Biondi-Santi's soft sell involves only a rare tasting or public appearance. He has reasoned correctly that he would get all the free publicity he needed by discreetly placing some well-aged bottles on the market at prices unheard of for Italian wine.

His 1983 list has the 1977 *riserva* at 44,000 lire[1] and ranges back through such memorable vintages as 1975 (73,000 lire), 1971 (90,000), 1955 (290,000), 1945 (590,000) and 1925 (3,300,000) to the historic 1891. At exchange rates quoted below, some of those old bottles reach triple and quadruple figures in sterling. And those are cellar prices, not retail (though discounts are offered for quantities). Biondi-Santi carries it off with such quiet poise that one suspects not so much a calculated stab at snob appeal as a heartfelt conviction that his wines are somehow worth that much.

But are they? Only those who buy them can really know, and I have not often counted myself among the buyers. Even if I could afford them, I might seek out better value in other Brunellos, yes, certain chiantis, Barolo, Barbaresco, not to mention Pétrus and Lafite. But that does not discount the grandeur of some Biondi-Santi bottles or their unique appeal to other palates. Nothing I have tasted since has equalled that 1964.

Other growers

Two other Montalcino estates – Fattoria dei Barbi of Francesca Colombini and Colle al Matrichese of the Costanti family – have earned solid reputations with wines crafted along similarly classical lines. But their reserves do not go back as far as Biondi-Santi's and only rarely have they approached his prices.

This old guard has been joined by a handful of not always rigidly tradition-

[1] Approximate rates of exchange in summer 1983: £ = 2,200 lire; $ = 1,400 lire.

Jacopo Biondi-Santi tastes
Greppo Brunello with his
father

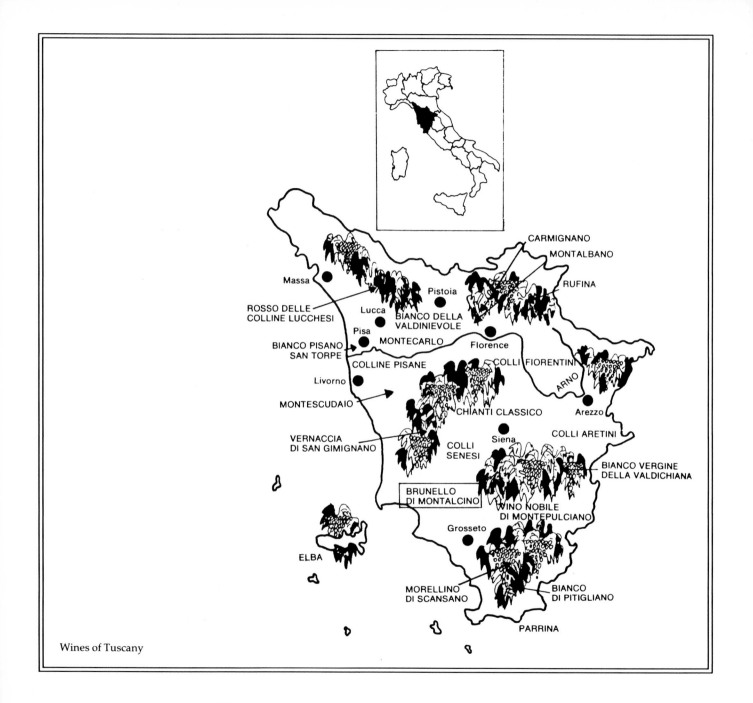

Wines of Tuscany

minded neighbours, some with admirable Brunello, some not. The most constantly good value over the last decade has come from Il Poggione, which shone even in 1972 and 1976, when most others failed. Signs of inherent class have been shown by Argiano, Camigliano, Canalicchio di Sopra, Col d'Orcia and Lisini, while Altesino and Tenuta Caparzo rate as most promising of the relative newcomers. Certain of future prominence are Castelgiocondo, Val di Suga and Villa Banfi, all backed by heavy investment.

Together these producers have issued enough wines of enough class to have convinced enough experts (non-Italian in the main) that Brunello di Montalcino is, indeed, Italy's worthiest appellation. And yet, as Brunello's stock has risen, I have found myself increasingly pressed to come to grips with this elusive aristocrat from Montalcino. Too many producers have issued too many bottles from too many vintages in recent times that have been in no way worthy of the name or the price.

That is not to deny the propensity for greatness in Montalcino's hills, already demonstrated in certain wines from those producers named. The zone has been noted for fine wines since the Middle Ages. But until Brunello came along the star was a sweet white from a local strain of *muscat* known as Moscadello, a wine being revived in a modern (lightly bubbly) context.

The vineyards

Within the extensive community lie some 800 hectares of vineyards designated for Brunello, all on slopes at between 800 and 1,600 feet, tapering towards the encircling valleys of the Asso, Orcia and Ombrone rivers, which merge and empty into the Tyrrhenian Sea 25 miles to the south-west. The tawny terrain consists mainly of clay mixed with schist, gravel, limestone or sand, rich in marl, as evidenced by the well-distributed remnants of seashells and fossils. The temperate Mediterranean climate of these hills favours slow, even ripening of grapes – *Brunello* and heavy recent plantings of *moscato, cabernet* and *chardonnay*.

Recent soil analysis shows at least as much promise in several vineyards not yet in full production as in proven plots. Much new planting has taken place on low hills in the south-west corner of the zone nearest the sea, around the localities of Sant'Angelo in Colle, Poggio alle Mura, Argiano, Camigliano and Castelgiocondo. Growers in this area, where ripening is more complete and humidity rarely a problem, speak disdainfully of the higher eastern slopes where Greppo and Barbi are located as the wrong side of the tracks. But in hot years, the upper levels boast wines that are more perfumed and less alcoholic. In the past, considerable shifting of grapes and wine took place, but in these days of new emphasis on special vineyards, estate bottling and individual integrity, it is hard to say how much of such beneficial blending is carried out.

A series of good to excellent crops from 1977 through 1982 was a boon to all Brunello producers, particularly those working with new vines, who easily outnumber the old. In fact, growth has been so rapid and change so radical in Montalcino's vineyards that Brunello must be considered not so much for what it has been as for what it seems destined to be.

DOC properties

Between 1970 and 1980, registered *denominazione di origine controllata* (DOC) properties increased from 42 to 93, hectares under vine from 103 to 687 and wine production from less than 3,000 hectolitres to more than 30,000 – enough for 4,000,000 bottles. Since 1980, the pace has actually quickened as new capital, much of it foreign, has been pumped into Montalcino's once bucolic wine industry. The limits of about 40,000 hectolitres should be reached late in this decade, though not all the wine will be sold as Brunello.

A secondary product of the same vines has just gained DOC status as Rosso di Montalcino, after being sold for years under the illegal appellation Rosso dai Vigneti di Brunello and other private names. Though not usually made from select grapes, this less expensive red, with little or no barrel age, can be superb when young. Over the years, I have had more enjoyment from this unpretentious *rosso* – especially from Il Poggione, with its unharnessed vigour and luscious ripe fruit flavours – than I have from a majority of the wizened veterans of mouldering wooden casks sold as Brunello di Montalcino.

The new-wave producers pay lip service to the Brunello legend because they recognise its value as a marketing tool, even if some scoff behind the scenes at the fairy-tale segments of the saga. Pragmatists (sometimes maddeningly so), as Italy's progressive oenologists tend to be, their answer to the challenge of selling premium wine at a profit in a world with the economic jitters is to make every phase of production as streamlined as it can be. In other words, to come up with the best possible wine in the shortest possible time, and to hell with the dust-covered myths.

Age of vines

The old guard will argue that it is heresy to presume that true Brunello can be extracted from young vines or hurried in any other stage of its development. Theirs is a product of love, patience, wisdom, acquired through the ages and passed down from father to son. Biondi-Santi uses only vines ten years or older for Brunello. His *riserva* gets five years in casks of Slavonian oak and more time in bottle before being sold. Buyers are advised to store the wine much longer in

The fortress of Montalcino – last refuge of the Republic of Siena till 1555

cool cellars and to open bottles a day ahead of time to let the wine breathe.

Progressives concede that old vines would be preferable, but by limiting yields and selecting carefully from the heartiest plants they can work with entirely satisfactory grapes. They might add that the true old Brunello came from vines grown in what Italians refer to so quaintly as 'promiscuous' culture, trained onto stunted trees placed there for the purpose and interspersed with olive trees and field crops. Old timers are the first to admit that such grapes had more substance, and that Brunello from their own specialised plots could never be quite the same.

Cask age

Another sore point is ageing. Progressives assert that it is purest folly to put a wine of any provenance into casks for four years (as required by the 'antiquated' rules). Even the mightiest of vintages will show signs of drying up, they say, while the old guard insists that long wood ageing is the *sine qua non* of Brunello's austerity, complexity and longevity.

The old Brunello is certain to be around for quite some time, though not so much to drink as to admire as an expensive antique. The emerging style falls somewhere between the severe *riserva* of Biondi-Santi and the opulent *rosso* of Il Poggione. The new Brunello will inevitably be a creature of stainless steel vats and smaller, newer barrels, such as the 225-litre French *barriques* which have been arriving in Montalcino with increasing regularity. Oenologists know that they will have to bend the rules until they manage to change them, but they are determined to make wines of more pronounced fruit, smoother, rounder texture and greater charm with the balance of components to uphold Brunello's reputation for ageing.

New wineries

In their drive to buck tradition, the progressives are relying heavily on science: in studies of soil, root stocks, plant density, and methods of training, pruning and fertilising. Some of their programmes call for irrigation and mechanical harvesting. The newer *cantine,* with their gleaming systems for crushing, vinifying and storage, are studies in *avant-garde* wine making. The epitome is the complex nearing completion in the southern part of the zone by the American giant Villa Banfi under the direction of Italy's most noted oenologist, Ezio Rivella, who goes about much of his business in a helicopter. With its prefabricated winery and miles of concrete poles, the Banfi operation resembles a vast swatch of California's Central Valley stretched across an ancient tapestry of Tuscan castles, villas and hilltop hamlets.

The contrasts in Montalcino today are more than just aesthetic. Still, the clash of interests between the established forces and the new has not developed as was feared. After some grumbling about multi-national giants and American capitalists (terms not easily digested in left-leaning Tuscany), the citizens of Montalcino put up none of the resistance they were so noted for in the past. 'After all', mused Communist Mayor Ilio Raffaelli about the latest invaders, 'they're bringing us money and jobs'.

Even Franco Biondo-Santi seems to have taken the incursion in his stride, seeing little threat to his own seemingly invincible status. He notes contentedly that Villa Banfi will devote most of its effort to bubbly Moscadello, California-style Cabernet and Chardonnay, while not adding significantly to the output of Brunello.

Banfi's Ezio Rivella admits that he does not see a terribly bright future for élite, expensive, hard-to-understand wines like Brunello. But he could not resist making some wine of the type from the brilliant 1981 and 1982 vintages from the firm's infant vines for Brunello. Rivella described the 1981 as 'by any laboratory measure as close to perfect as a red wine can be'. Not only that, he reassured, it smells and tastes that good. Would he put it in a wooden cask for four years? 'Would you?' he countered with an inscrutable grin.

Even space-age wine makers know the value of a little old-fashioned mystique.

A small hill-town near Montalcino

Twelve Bordeaux Châteaux

Described by Hugh Johnson and lithographed by Charles Mozley

There are *châteaux* great and small all over France, but the notion of the wine *château* is unique to Bordeaux. In Bordeaux a *château* is not a castle or even an old manor. It is simply a wine-producing estate – the whole unit: the land, its vines, its buildings, its traditions and techniques, its vats and machinery, its workers, its microclimate and its philosophy.

The central feature is of course the land. Just how important the very soil is has been established beyond doubt by the scarcely altered validity of a classification which began to emerge 200 years ago. Men, methods and materials have all changed since Lafite, Latour and the rest were recognised as the best *châteaux* – yet their sites still maintain their pre-eminence.

If it were only a matter of the land, however, *châteaux* would disappear more frequently than they do, for the boundaries of holdings are not as immutable as one might imagine. A *château* can gain or lose or exchange a big block of vineyard and still keep its identity. What ultimately counts is the stability of the whole complex: the fact that the same estate, be it bigger or smaller, well run or badly run, is still in business, making wine in its own subtly different way.

The symbol of this stability is the *château* – the owner's house, which has the courtesy title of 'castle' whether it is a mansion or a shed. The aspirations and achievements of the owner are summed up in the house he builds as the headquarters and symbol of his estate.

The history of the estates of Bordeaux, the relative fortunes of one district and another, the rise of one social class after another, the amassing of millions and the decline of proud houses can be read in the buildings that stand witness among the vines.

It is not so long a history as one might suppose. The Bordeaux which supplied its mother country, England, with claret during the 300 years of English rule was not organised in substantial estates making identifiable wines. The unit was the peasant's patch; its production a tun or two of anonymous lightweight wine made to be drunk up before the next harvest. The lord of the manor doubtless drank the best and was content with his taxes levied on the rest.

Not until the later years of the 16th century did new-style landowners emerge who amassed larger holdings of vineyard land under their direct control. The process began in the Graves, just south of the city of Bordeaux, the old heart of the Aquitaine vineyards. The first *château* to be established on this basis was Haut-Brion, created by a politician-lawyer, a member of the principal monied class in Bordeaux from the 16th century until well into the 18th. The manor house he built still stands substantially as he left it. Haut-Brion remained unusual, and pre-eminent for nearly a century before the 'fury of planting' swept into the Médoc and the great familiar *château* names of Pauillac, Margaux and St.-Julien began to appear.

The Médoc in the 16th century was described as a wild and solitary place, on the road to nowhere. A line of forts along the Gironde estuary gave it military importance, but there were few (if any) vineyards; the country was either forest or marsh.

The draining of the marshes by Dutch engineers in the 17th century was the first step in creating the great vineyard which covers most of the riverside Médoc today. They dug or enlarged the *jalles* which flow from the wooded back country into the Gironde. The old catch phrase of the Médoc has always been that the best vineyards 'look at the river'. The better drainage of the riverside slopes was the reason. But to 'look at' a *jalle* was almost as good. The correlation between the best growths and the drainage system is strikingly clear to this day.

Bordeaux was immensely prosperous in the 18th century, as its splendid streets and squares of the period still testify. Colonial trade made new millionaires to add to the aristocracy of lawyers who were already in the ascendant. To grow wine was not only profitable; the possession of a vineyard estate gave dignity and social standing. In the early years of the 18th century the vineyard acreage of Bordeaux more than doubled. The special relationship between the investors of Bordeaux and the Médoc in particular remains to this day.

The only factor holding back the 'civilisation' of the Médoc in the sense of house building and permanent residence, was the lack of a road. In 1780 Pauillac was still the end of the rough road north from Bordeaux. The only important estates were former feudal domains, not wine properties: houses like Issan, Margaux and Beychevelle. They had their own ports. The new proprietors in the main restricted themselves to building lodges or pavilions, not to live in but for directing their properties and entertaining their friends at vintage time.

The most popular model of pavilion or small country house was the traditional *chartreuse* – the Gironde's name for a long low building rather after the manner of a railway carriage, single-storied and one room deep, sometimes with cross wings and occasionally with an extra storey at the ends. The Carthusian monks (*chartreuse* means charterhouse – a Carthusian establishment) settled deep in the country and hence one's country retreat was a *'chartreuse'*. The Provençal *mas* is the same sort of thing. Near St.-Malo in Normandy the term is *malouinière*. Clearly it was cheaper to build a single storey: less foundations were called for – especially on swampy ground, which was common in the Gironde. The low houses of Bordeaux itself, however, are said to have a different origin; they were grouped round the old fortress, the Château Trompette, and were built low to allow its guns to fire over their roofs.

Right up to the Revolution the Bordeaux vineyard (above all the Médoc) grew and prospered, the peasant tenants growing inexorably poorer as their noble masters grew richer. When the Marquis de Ségur, owner of both Lafite and Latour, died in 1755 it was found that these two estates had been bringing in 100,000 *livres* a year, of which 60 per cent was net profit.

The Revolution brought the first age of expansion to an end, but in itself upset the pattern of ownership only where the proprietor fled the country. The estates of *emigrés* were confiscated and sold. Twenty-five years of war and upheaval on the other hand were bound to cause changes. For many they created new opportunities – they saw some curious new landlords appear; the men who brought Lafite and Beychevelle among them. The early years of the Revolution indeed were a time of intensive building activity as landlords improved what they saw as their safest asset – their land. On the whole the old families weathered the storm, surviving a generation of challenging years to emerge in the new age of expansion which followed the fall of Napoleon.

Suprisingly, the grandest *château* of all, Château Margaux, dates from these very years of stress. There is confidence enough in the tall portico which dwarfs almost every other building in the Médoc.

From the 1820s onwards Parisian, English, American and Dutch investors descended on Bordeaux in an unending stream. The extraordinary *jeu d' esprit* of Cos d'Estournel belongs to the 1830s. *Château* building began again in earnest in the 1840s. The First Empire is represented by relatively few monuments among the vineyards, but the eclectic mid-Victorian style of the age of Louis-Philippe merging into the Second Empire is practically the trade mark of the Médoc.

The feeling of the period is best summed up by such mansions as Pichon-Lalande, Pichon-Baron, and Château Palmer. They suggest, above all, a man of commerce proud to have become a landowner, and groping for some worthy symbol of his new identity. Some mercifully had a sense of proportion (even humour) to guide them. Others did not. But every pocket proprietor did his best to follow suit. The golden years before the phylloxera of the early 80s gave the growers deep purses. It was a poor *vigneron* indeed who could not afford at least one turret tacked on to his farmhouse to lend credence to the title of *château*.

The Médoc may be said to have reached its climax as an industrial and social entity in the Second Empire. A succession of Paris bankers led by Aguado, Marquis de las Marismas, at Château Margaux, had bought estates and embellished them. An account of the vintage at Beychevelle, the property of the great banker Fould, sets the scene: after a vast lunch and cigars on the terrace the party strolled among the outbuildings to watch the harvesters at their cabbage soup (which was good, the writer noted, and full of bits of meat). Then rides or drives up and down the rows of vines – *'à côté de nous passe la calèche de la toute gracieuse baronne Gustave de Rothschild et de son mari . . . la jolie famille de M. Johnston . . . Pereires . . . Duchâtel . . . comte d'Aguado . . . Prince et Princesse Murat . . . les Ségur . . . les d'Erlanger . . . c'est le Faubourg St. Honoré, ce sont les Champs Elysées prolongés, c'est Paris.'*

The euphoria, and the *château* building ended with the coming of phylloxera. The plague came to Bordeaux in 1879. For a full decade the growers fought it with every means their imaginations could suggest, from fumigation of the soil to flooding the vineyards. On top of phylloxera in the early 80s came mildew. Meanwhile France entered a period of slump, and the price of wine fell disastrously. The banker-investors found they were in a more serious business than they had bargained for.

Although the recovery from phylloxera was rapid once the remedy (of grafted vines) was found, and mildew soon met its match in copper sulphate, the midsummer mood had left the Médoc, not to return for three generations. And *château* building in the old style was over – for ever.

The rise of St.-Emilion and Pomerol comes almost as a footnote to this story. Long-established and excellent though their vineyards were, in 1880 their wines were still virtually unknown to the outside world. The *bourgeois* of Libourne, their market town, invested in them just as the *bordelais* invested in the Médoc. But Libourne was not Bordeaux: the wealth, the worldliness and above all the contacts with the outside world were missing. Thus the Libourne wine district missed the great age of estate building when small parcels were amalgamated wholesale into huge properties. Holdings stayed relatively small, and houses on them remained in keeping.

The 20th century began on a sombre note for the Bordeaux estates. Production was high; prices and morale were low. The Great War added to their difficulties. American Prohibition followed on its tail. To make matters worse there was an extraordinary run of poor vintages, with scarcely a good one between 1900 and 1920.

The early 20s saw some superb claret made, and for a while the gloom seemed to lighten. But in 1929 came the slump, followed by an austere decade ending with the Second World War. It was the 1950s before the *châteaux* began to climb out of the slough of despond. The 40s had ended with three excellent vintages. Early in the 50s profits began to return. From 1960 onwards America, virtually no market at all since 1919, began to buy claret. A new age of investment opened such as Bordeaux had not seen since phylloxera.

But whereas the investors of the Second Empire built themselves *châteaux*, the new interest in Bordeaux was in wine technology. It was in the *chai* and the *cuvier* where the wine is made that the money was spent.

As a result the Gironde vineyard remains remarkably unaltered in appearance since the great days of display. What has changed in the last 90 years has been below the surface. Bordeaux, as expressed in its architecture, is still in another world – a world which claret drinkers return to in their dreams.

Château Mouton-Rothschild *is essentially the work of one man, without a doubt the most distinguished wine grower of our time: Baron Philippe de Rothschild. He inherited the estate with its run-down reputation and modest dwelling in 1922. Since then he has applied himself ceaselessly to creating a first growth and a fitting mansion – a building of style, beauty and even grandeur, formed from the old stable range. Mouton's famous art museum, is all of a piece with the house, the chais, the cellars and the vineyards: the masterwork of a man of matchless taste, energy and imagination.*

Château d'Issan *is too pretty to be typical of the Médoc. It is almost like an English country house, a miniature Wilton, with its airy symmetrical façade unburdened by the towering range of roofs of most big French houses. Although its moat sleepily registers a long-forgotten state of warlike alert, nowhere in Bordeaux feels remoter or more peaceful. It lies low in the riverside meadows, where cows huddle in the shade of poplars, where it seems perpetual afternoon. Its vineyards on the gravel slope above, though smaller than those of the most famous châteaux, produce a lovely gentle and typical Margaux.*

Vieux Château Certan. *Pomerol has no natural beauty to catch the eye. Anthing more than a mere farmhouse stands out as a mansion in this flat landscape. Vieux Château Certan, the 16th century manor house of one of the oldest estates, scarcely expresses wealth ('Certan' originally meant desert). Yet there is a memory of the Médoc chartreuse in the low centre block between the towers. And in its Belgian ownership over the last 70 years it has established itself as an almost Médoc style château – even to the firm style of its wine.*

Château Palmer *is the very model of a modern Médoc château – modern, that is, in the Deuxième Empire heyday of the genre. The banker, Isaac Pereire, precisely hit the gay eclecticism and happy harmony of a style that expresses summer holidays in long frocks. Basically, the house is a simple bourgeois box, but a distinct memory of Azay-le-Rideau is evoked by the pretty neo-renaissance turrets and the steep roof, as sharp and shiny as a blade. Three flags, for its French, Dutch and English owners, gaily greet the visitor from the rooftop as he drives through Cantenac. Palmer in recent years has often challenged first growths in quality.*

Château Ducru-Beaucaillou *creates an impression of awesome size. There is something of the grand spa hotel in the upreared pavilion at either end of the long central block. Its extra dimensions it owes principally to a housing problem: it belonged to a man who had 14 children. And it stands, unusually, over its chais. If the owners since 1941, the Borie family, are more restrained in their progeny, they are more than ever successful in their cru. Ducru today stands high among the proudest of the Médoc second growths.*

Château Margaux. *The Médoc only reaches a ducal level of splendour once: at Château Margaux. All country whimsy, all flirtation with a gothic past here give way to neo-classical purity. Margaux is Athenian: scoff who dares. As elsewhere, Bordeaux lawyers and Paris bankers were behind all this grandeur. At Margaux the property fully merits the display: its stony soil gives Bordeaux's most finely fragrant wine. Happily a trough in its fortunes gave place, in 1975, to new investment and the reinstatement of its splendid name as the queen of the first growths.*

Château Pétrus *rejoices in its anomaly: the most modest of châteaux with the ne plus ultra of red wine. It has no great estate, still less a heraldic history. It emerged from obscurity only a century ago, the home of a bourgeois gentleman who loved good wine – and whose few acres on the undramatic brow of Pomerol proved capable of making the best. It was the local hotelière, Madame Loubat, in the 1930s who made it famous. Today it is run by the first family of Pomerol, the Moueix, with solemn perfectionism – as befits the trustees of a famous jewel.*

Château Langoa-Barton. *One of the most elegantly French of all Médoc châteaux belongs perversely to the most remarkable dynasty of foreigners in Bordeaux: the Anglo-Irish Barton family. The lovely stone chartreuse, lofty on a terrace above its cellars, has been Barton property since 1821, and the base for their two estates: the consistently brilliant second growth, Léoville, and the third growth, Langoa. If there is any outward sign of Englishness it is in the garden, where roses billow and cascade in a manner they must have learnt at English hands.*

Château Cheval-Blanc *is no less historic than many a Médoc estate; only, in the rural retirement of St.-Emilion less of a showplace and more of a family home. The Fourcaud-Lussacs have owned parts of the property for 150 years, and built the château in 1860; a pleasant house rather than an impressive one; cream-washed, orderly, neo-classical without excess, well-planted with screening trees that now, a century later, give it the dignity its superlative wine deserves.*

Château Lagrange *stands in the back country of St.-Julien, away from the riverside, like a haunted palace in a fairy tale. To a romantic it has perhaps the most powerful presence of any Médoc château. Its vast park, its overgrown lake, its endless barns and stables all speak of departed glory. Lagrange has had a disturbed history. It was embroiled in the Revolution, and has twice belonged to Spanish families, once to an Englishman. Now once again it fortunes are changing – perhaps to restore its plump and earthy claret into a wine of appropriately haunting beauty.*

Château La Mission-Haut-Brion. *The name commemorates the preaching Lazarite fathers of the 16th century, vowed to poverty, who chose their land so well that it sold, after their dispossession by the Revolution, for 100,000 livres of silver. The gravel site they planted abuts the great Château Haut-Brion. Nothing is left of their buildings, but subsequent owners have chosen to commemorate them by building a chapel and filling their new and comfortable house with ecclesiastical objects. Subsequent owners are better remembered by the quality of the wine of the vineyard they planted.*

Château Cos-d'Estournel. *Nobody looking at the bizarre chai can help wondering whether M d'Estournel had been to Brighton and fallen in love with the Prince Regent's Pavilion. France has no other folly like it. Jeu d'esprit is probably a better word, for this is no pure folly but a working wine warehouse dressed in the finery of the east. Its history is as calm as its looks are bizarre. Under its present director, Bruno Prats, the wine itself has become history. Cos today is at the very summit of its reputation for manly, beautifully-fashioned, yes, perhaps opulent, claret.*

Wines and Fashion
Some reflections in a glass
Serena Sutcliffe, MW

Social historians sometimes like to link fashion in clothes with the economic conditions prevailing in a country. Much was made of Dior's New Look after the Second World War, which was his way of saying farewell to austerity. The luxury and extravagance of great swirling skirts, with their greedy use of material, caused an outburst from Sir Stafford Cripps, then president of the Board of Trade, but it seemed as if the consumers themselves were ready to embrace frivolity.

Now even economists, that most staid breed of men, link fashion with the relative prosperity of a country. Robert Beckman in his book *The Downwave* elaborates a theory that healthy, growing economies engender daring, even sexually provocative clothes, while a depressing economic picture produces prudence in dress, illustrated by low hemlines and high necklines. The most up-to-date manifestation of this, apparently, is the arrival of the latest collections in France, with their swooping hemlines, just as President Mitterand's Socialist régime introduces austerity measures of a somewhat Draconian nature.

I am not sure if this shows us yet again that the French are our arbiters of fashion, or that they lead in political economic thought, but I do know that it is easier to manipulate hemlines than styles in wine. Nevertheless, wines tend to follow certain trends for a period of time, before turning in another direction and achieving different ends. Nature, in the form of climate, obviously has an influence over the type of wine made, as indeed it can in the realm of clothes (Moscow fashion shows have more furs than bikinis), but man and his machines wield a mighty power.

In the spring of 1983, a few privileged people had time to ponder this at a vividly instructive tasting put on by Monsieur Louis Vialard, the proprietor and wine maker at Château Cissac, that excellent *Grand Bourgeois Exceptionnel* of the Haut-Médoc. The specific aim of the tasting was to observe the two quite different styles of wine made over the last two decades, from the 1959 vintage to the 1979, to pinpoint the vintage where the style changed, and to say which style we preferred.

It was quite easy to see where the style changed – the cut-off point was the 1970 vintage – but more difficult to reason why. There was no doubt that the wines were bigger up to, and including, 1970, with the more recent vintages more supple, less fleshy, and quicker maturing. Louis allowed the buzz of suppositions to simmer down, and then gave us three lucid reasons. It should be emphasised that these were the deciding factors for changing the style of Cissac, in the heart of Bordeaux's Médoc, but they would not necessarily have been as decisive, or had the same effect, in other parts of the world.

During the 60s, the policy at Cissac was to add some *vin de presse*, while the wines from the 70s were the result of the free-run wine (*vin de goutte*), with no added press wine. *Vin de presse* inevitably contributes an element of hardness or backbone to a wine, with a certain astringency in youth which mellows with age. Free-run wine is more supple, with much less tannin. In his *Connaissance et Travail du Vin*, a crystal clear book on wine making if ever there was one, Professeur Emile Peynaud shows a fascinating table charting the differences between *vin de goutte* and *vin de presse*. It emerges that the press wine is more concentrated in all the elements (types of acidity, extract, tannins, colour) than the free-run wine, with the exception of the alcohol level, and when it comes from good grape varieties, in fine wine regions, its addition to the *grand vin* is beneficial.

The second cause of a change of style at Cissac was an increased proportion of *cabernet-franc* in the vineyard. While a vital ingredient in St.-Emilion and Pomerol, for example, the inclusion of this grape variety in the hinterland of the Médoc could be less advisable. According to Louis Vialard, at Cissac the *cabernet-franc* does not give much colour or body to the resulting wine, contributing a slightly 'diluted' effect in comparison with the definite, firm *cabernet-sauvignon*, which will replace in large part the *cabernet-franc* in the years to come. Having

As seen in Vogue. Dior's
New Look sketched at
Maxim's by Nobili, 1947

said this, it is worth noting that Château Cissac already has a fair amount of *cabernet-sauvignon* (vineyard proportions are 75 per cent *cabernet*, of which 80 per cent is *cabernet-sauvignon*, 20 per cent *merlot* and 5 per cent *petit verdot*), and even the more supple style of the 70s reflects this.

The third change of tactic employed at Cissac which contributed to the two distinct styles of wine made was the picking date for the grapes. During the 60s, Louis tended to pick earlier rather than later, thereby maintaining a higher acidity, which is a great asset in wines intended for longer ageing. During the 70s, the picking was generally done later, consequently resulting in riper grapes with lower acidity. This naturally contributes to the wines' quality of being 'accessible' younger, softer and initially more flattering to the palate.

The chips were down, and we had to plump for one style or another. In spite of the great attraction, fruitiness and *gouleyant* qualities of the wines of the 70s, I was a push-over for the more robust, powerful, mouth-filling wines of the 60s. Naturally, one had to wait to see them at their best, but if that means savouring the rich complexities of the 1959, the 1961, and the 1962, patience is no difficult thing. The 1964 and 1966 were also superb, and one was amazed at the youthful presumption of the 1960, which just would not withdraw into the background and be ignored, even amongst the stars.

It would seem, however, that the more normal direction of affairs is towards wines which are more supple, quicker maturing and easy to comprehend. The danger is that, while undoubtedly delicious, they can manifest a certain *passe-partout* style. Not only does this render blind tastings more tricky, but one does miss the 'highs', even if not regretting the 'lows'.

In spite of the comparative short life of the Californian wine growing industry, it has already passed through many phases. It currently seems to be opting for a less massive style of wine making than was evidenced in the mid-70s – winds of change blow fast and furious on the west coast. The reasons for this change in emphasis, if not a complete about-turn, may stem partly from criticisms of lack of subtlety and refinement which the European camp were happy to throw across the Atlantic, but I would tend to think it was more an internal realisation that big is not necessarily beautiful. Perhaps it has something to do with the brisk, sporty life style now adopted by so many Americans – track-suit culture. You cannot down a whopping 14 per cent alcohol Cabernet-Sauvignon before jogging down the beach at Malibu, or dashing off to a work-out studio with a film star!

While all wines 'made in America' do not conform to the rigours of 'light wine', with its low alcohol and calories, there has been a gentle scaling down of

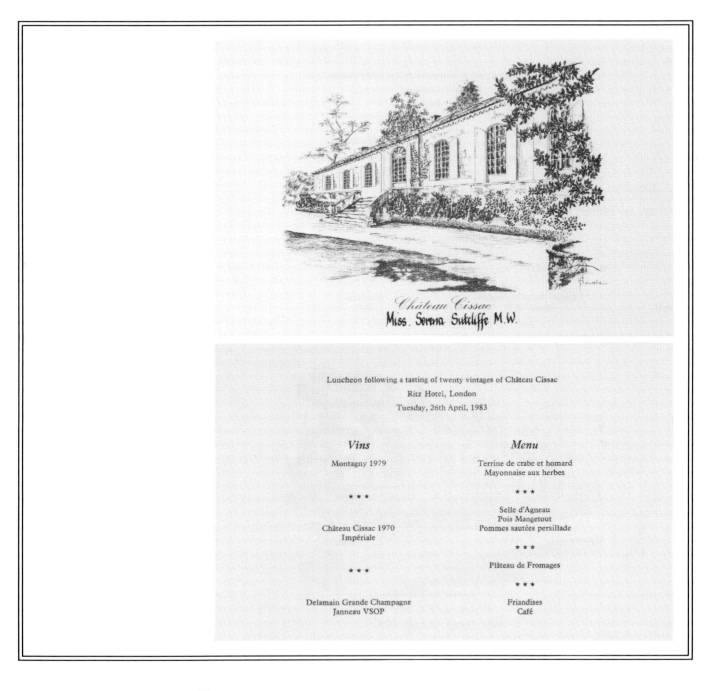

Château Cissac

Miss Serena Sutcliffe M.W.

Luncheon following a tasting of twenty vintages of Château Cissac

Ritz Hotel, London

Tuesday, 26th April, 1983

Vins	*Menu*
Montagny 1979	Terrine de crabe et homard Mayonnaise aux herbes
★ ★ ★	★ ★ ★
	Selle d'Agneau Pois Mangetout
Château Cissac 1970 Impériale	Pommes sautées persillade
	★ ★ ★
★ ★ ★	Plâteau de Fromages
	★ ★ ★
Delamain Grande Champagne Janneau VSOP	Friandises Café

peak alcohol levels in the top categories. Even more, there has been a rethinking of policy on whether 'one hundred per cent is beautiful' in the matter of grape varieties. When California began concentrating on the top French *cépages,* it was thought that a single noble grape variety would make more impressive wine than a blend. They were indeed impressive, but they were also one-dimensional, which ultimately leads to a dull wine. So, now, the *cabernet-sauvignon* is often tempered with the *merlot,* and the *sauvignon-blanc* is enhanced by the *sémillon,* and I, for one, think that more complex tastes are emerging.

Changing styles also lead to diversity of choice and, for anyone remotely interested in expanding the role of the taste buds, this can only be exciting. Comparing the big, buttery Chardonnays of Chalone and Chateau Montelena with the more floral styles of John Shafer or Charles Ortman, or the Sauvignon-Blanc of the latter with the more 'French' Dry Creek, or again with the fuller, wood-aged Mondavi or Sterling versions, is an education in itself. Chateau St.-Jean and Joseph Phelps might make late-harvested Rieslings which are difficult to tell apart, but the great, firm Robert Young Chardonnays of the former are light years away from the elegant creations at Phelps.

In our new-found appreciation that there is more to wine than full-frontal impact combined with massive back-up, there seems to be a more intelligent awareness of the marvellous drinking qualities of wines coming from houses once deemed 'unfashionable'. The old-established families in California, who always made good wine at fair prices but which did not catch the headlines with monotonous insistence, still give us balanced wines which one can drink all the time. A harmonious Merlot from Louis Martini or a Cabernet Sauvignon from Parducci can teach a hundred lessons to some new wineries surviving more on media brouhaha than consistent, dependable quality. When I first went to California, I was not aware of the 'snob' aspect of certain, high-spending estates, and judged wines as I tasted them, for sheer drinkability – perhaps this neglected quality is now coming back? And if subtlety is now the order of the day, it surely must be the hour for the emergence of a small winery like Kalin Cellars, the creator, amongst other things, of a Pinot Noir the like of which I did not expect to see in California during my lifetime.

There is a taste which really seems to be going out of fashion, and that is volatile acidity. Two decades ago, when I first, consciously, began to taste wines (as opposed to unconscious swilling), there was a great deal of it about, especially in the red wines of France and Italy. At that time, I could not identify it, but just knew that I thoroughly disliked that harsh, hard note in a wine, which often seemed to be accompanied by a deep, tempting colour. I then went to France for some years, and seemed not to find it so often – even less so in a sojourn in Finland, where the state monopoly has tight quality control on imported liquids. However, when I returned to Britain, I was once again assailed by this noxious property in wine, never more so than when kind people were opening their cellars of claret and burgundy for me, often London-bottled, and often from the vintages of the 40s and 50s.

Of course, no one had the cellar equipment then to cope with years like 1947, when the temperatures soared. Without cooling possibilities, the 1982s would have been like that. Cleanliness was also more haphazard, and the generous addition of *vin de presse* did not help matters, as it always has more volatile acidity than free-run wine. The result was that there was a certain 'English palate' which had grown accustomed to both the smell and taste of our old friend VA, and it had to be weaned away from love of bacteria! Initially, as wines became more healthy, there were rumblings that they did not have the same 'character' as of old, but now new fruit and charm have emerged through the masking veil of volatile and we have embarked on an era of purity where wines are concerned.

If proof were needed that the British have turned their backs on volatile acidity, it would be in the way they rejected Barolos from Piemonte when they first started appearing in the sceptred isle. The taste simply was not appreciated, and as most Barolos being sold up to the mid-70s were liberally laced with high volatile, partly due to the over-lengthy wood ageing, one can only deduce that it was this which did not appeal. Now this fault has largely been corrected in these very fine wines, sales of Barolo are noticeably higher and people are at last aware of the *real* taste of top quality Nebbiolo.

Drinking an Ausone 1877 the other day, I could not help toying with the theory that the wines of old had a higher residual sugar than they do today. There is no doubt that this stupendous wine had a glorious, sweetish finish, completely obviating any imbalance that otherwise might have been there with age. This was sheer finesse, lacy, seductive charm and lingering fruit. Ian Maxwell Campbell, in his entrancing *Wayward Tendrils of the Vine* (1947), waxes lyrical about the sweetness in the clarets of this epoch: 'One of the outstanding characteristics of the '75s was their extraordinary sweetness. We never seem to see it in the clarets of nowadays and it is one of the first attributes I look for. You will still find it, or remember it, in the older vintages, such as '58, and '64, '65 and '68, '70, '71, '74, '75 and '77 and, to a lesser degree, in '78, but thereafter one almost looks for it in vain in most vintages.'

Do we make our wines today too dry, and when they are as old as this, will they have that soaring, ripe quality, or will they finish harsh and acid? The same ideas were running through the mind of Christian Moueix, as we drank long and reverently, the ideas becoming more expansive as the evening wore on. The Bordeaux wines of 1982 might well have a touch more residual sugar left in them than, say, in 1978, whether deliberately engineered or as the natural result of one of the ripest years ever. It was, in fact, quite difficult to finish the fermentations of the 1982s, and often extra yeasts had to be added in order that they could finish 'cleanly'. It is certainly true to say that it would be dangerous to allow fermentations to stop before they have completed and to foster unstable levels of sugar which could turn out to be time bombs in the bottle, but a touch less asperity in a wine from a naturally ripe year could well give us bottles which will last 100 years or more.

Is there now a genuine fashion for wines with more than a touch of carbonic gas in them? The vast armies of Lambrusco lovers in America would agree, as would the citizens of Modena, Parma and Bologna, who drink fizzy Lambrusco of rather a different nature. Undoubtedly, the massive sales of fruity or sugary bubbly drinks have encouraged the love of fizz, but will this extend to a general tendency to bottle dry white wines with a marked level of gas in them? Many Italian fresh whites now sport a degree of bubble, and when it is kept low, it can be attractive and sprightly. But if it is high enough to be really noticed, it is usually too high. When there is more than a slight prickle on the tongue, and the wine fizzes actively in the mouth, it masks some of the bouquet and taste along the way.

The fashion would seem unhappily to have temporarily disappeared for those exquisite examples of German wine making skill – Riesling Prädikat wines from the top estates of the Rhine and the Mosel. It seems inexplicable, as the taste for sweet Sauternes and Barsac appears to be creeping back (now that we have learned to drink them with *foie gras*, as well as airy orange mousse and bread-and-butter pudding), but that unrivalled combination of lusciousness and balancing acidity, which is the hallmark of great Riesling, is still appreciated by far too few people.

The fabled wines of the 20s were kept in wood for as long as four to five years, and they naturally were far drier than wines of today, except in the most extreme cases of ripeness. After the Second World War, the Germans had a craving for sugar, and the technology of *süss* (or sweet) reserve developed. That has remained with us, and is often something of an exaggeration, with a banal degree of sugar overriding all. But when the sweetness comes from ripe conditions, and the wines are bottled young, as they are, of course, nowadays,

1883 or 1983?

there develops in the bottle that searingly lovely battle between uncloying sweetness and fruity acidity which can only result in victory for the taster. Miss these wines at your peril.

Finally, there seems to be a taste which may just be lost for ever, and nothing could be more tragic in the vinous world. This is the salty-rich-tangy *austerity* of true *amontillado* sherry, that which is aged *fino* and not sweetened, sickly boredom-in-a-bottle. Whether the exigencies of modern cost accounting have been more pronounced down in Jerez than anywhere else I do not know, but I suspect that the Spaniards succumbed to the wheedling of the cheap wine merchants in a way which they should not have done, and came 'down to a price', with a crash, as it turned out. Whatever the reasons, the result is catastrophic, and to those who can lay their hands on stocks of genuine, nutty *amontillado*, I can only say, go forth and buy.

In these days of recession, combined with technological advance and an awareness of our capacity to improve ourselves as never before, or to destroy ourselves totally, what are the wines of our age? Perhaps it would be more apposite to ask, what are the wines which will soothe us on our way?

I would like to think that the Bordeaux 1982s are the wines to give us hope and ultimate pleasure. They combine the abundance and generosity of nature with the skill and technical intelligence of man. As far as fashions in clothes go with wine, what will they bring in their wake? The Edwardians had Paul Poiret and his Russian extravaganzas to brighten up the dreary vintages from 1910 onwards, the shimmering colours of Fortuny brought those glittering vintages of the 20s, while that epitome of elegance in a wine, 1953, just had to be represented by Balenciaga.

Now, with the 1982s, we have opulence and classic beauty. Will we turn to Yves St. Laurent, with his flamboyance, jewel colours and *éclat*, or will we stay with the timeless line and structure of Armani and Versace? After a heady tasting of these wines in barrel, my heart is with the textured, tactile clothes of Missoni – but I suspect that, after I have paid the prices for these glorious wines, *haute couture* will be irrelevant and I will happily drink them in rags.

The International Wine & Food Society 1933–1983 . . .

No one during the last half century has had a greater influence on gastronomy than the man portrayed above. André Simon was a prolific writer, still widely read though he died 13 years ago. But his influence has prevailed more powerfully through the Wine and Food Society that he founded in 1933, and its *Journal* that he edited for 30 years.

Within a year of its foundation, André's missionary journeys had extended the Society to the United States. After the war he was to take it to Australasia and South Africa. The International Wine & Food Society, as it is now called, has 200 branches in 35 countries, and individual members in 15 more. Though the membership is chiefly English speaking, there are branches in Belgium, France, West Germany, Hong Kong, Japan, Kowloon, Malaysia, Mexico, the Scandinavian countries, Singapore and Tahiti.

Enthusiastically-attended international conventions have been held in Chicago, London and Torquay, Paris, California, London again, Australia and now this year in British Columbia.

How, it may be asked, does the Society compare in its golden jubilee year with that of 50 years ago? No organisation remains the same for half a century, but healthy ones adapt themselves. It must be remembered that the Society was born in the great depression, when even the most famous restaurateurs were delighted to serve a dinner for many covers at prices that now seem ridiculous. Fine, mature wines were then very inexpensive. Inflation has changed all that. Everyone eats less, and most people drink more simply.

There are still many grand meals, but there are also simple ones. Educational functions have developed. Some meetings take place in members' homes. Wines that have become too expensive to drink can still be tasted. Sights may have to be lowered, but not standards. The gospel of good eating and sound drinking continues to be propagated as the Society passes into its second half century. Members can still, in the words of their founder, thank *le bon Dieu pour toutes les bonnes choses qu'il veut bien nous donner.*

H. W. Yoxall

A Memorable Meal, described by André Simon in the Journal of the Wine & Food Society, as it was called in those days

The place: 32 Montpelier Square.
The date: 6 December 1935.
The host: Guy Knowles.
The guests: J. E. Hutton, Gerald Kelly, Lewis C. Loyd, H. Rossiter and André L. Simon

The fare: Rougets, Pâté de gibier, Filet de boeuf, Bouchées au fromage, Dessert.
The wines: 1904 Cramant, 1911 Château Ausone, 1899 Château Pichon-Longueville, 1864 Château Lafite (magnum), 1870 Grand Fine Champagne Normandin.

Who asked if there ever had been a meal that deserved to be called perfect? Here is a perfect meal. Not *the* perfect meal, because perfection has so many forms, and it is quite possible for other meals to be perfect, and yet entirely different, from this perfect specimen of a perfect dinner. First of all the company: six men old enough to know and young enough to love that which is good and beautiful, terms which are interchangeable in all else but woman. The fare: simple, of the finest quality and perfectly cooked. The home-made pâté quite a 'high spot', as they say in New York, a most fascinating alloy of grouse, partridge and woodcock. Last, and by no means least, the wines: shades of Saintsbury! What wines! And how perfectly tuned, how beautifully set! The first one was one of those pure white grape champagnes, not sparkling, but just lively or *crémant*, which are so fascinating, and so rare. It had stood its thirty years' bottle confinement admirably and showed no trace of fatigue whatever. It put the red mullet to bed with grace and finality before we approached the two wonderful clarets, so nobly supported by the best pâté de gibier I can recollect. The Ausone was the *Grand Seigneur* and the Pichon the *Grande Dame*, softer, more bending, with a sweeter bouquet than the Ausone, which had a more dynamic personality and a richer robe. The Ausone was perhaps the more admirable of the two: the Pichon the more lovable.

And then came the climax: a perfect magnum of Lafite 1864. Praise be to the oak which produced the cork that did so well by the wine under its keeping for so many years. The wine was superb. It had not been bottled at the Château, but in Scotland, and in a Scotch magnum with a glass button blown in the glass, below the shoulder, with the name 'Lafite' and the date 1864 clean cut. And when, just in a quiet and 'by the way' tone, our host informed us that it had come from the late Professor George Saintsbury's cellar, the news seemed to put the loud pedal upon the bouquet of this wonderful wine. It reminded me of the Lafite 1858 which I drank at Versailles with the great Pasteur's daughter, son-in-law and grandson, a bottle left from some that the Rothschilds had given Pasteur for his research work on fermentation. A glass of Normandin 1870 brought this perfect dinner to a perfect finish.

A.L.S.

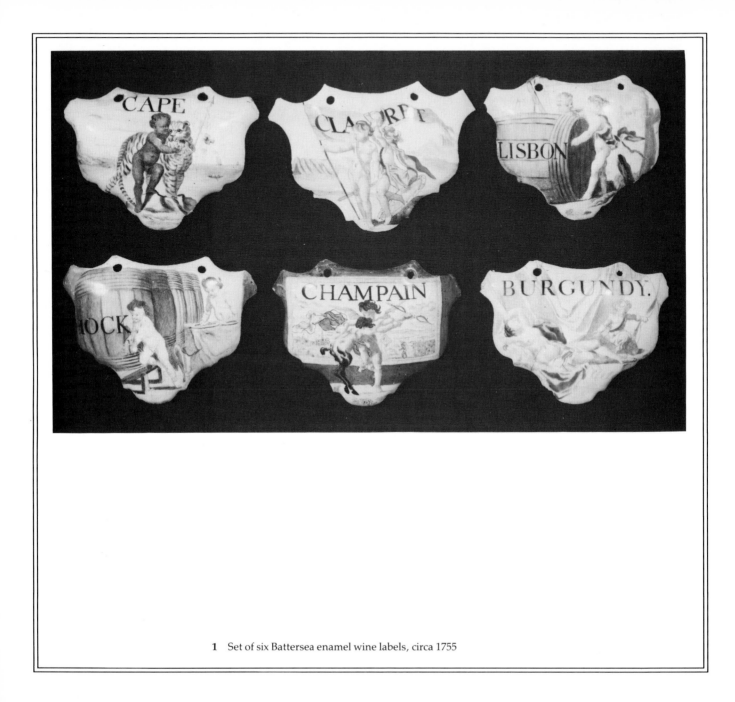

1 Set of six Battersea enamel wine labels, circa 1755

Wine labels
Bernard M. Watney, FSA

The origins

It is probable that wine labels, like postage stamps, were first introduced in Britain. Certainly during the eighteenth century, many more wine labels were produced in the British Isles than elsewhere, suggesting that we enjoyed a greater variety of wines than they did in other countries. In the wine-growing areas of Europe, the local wine was almost invariably drunk in preference to any other, even as it is today; it would not often be treated with the same ceremony or need to be differentiated among numerous imported beverages. In the latter part of the seventeenth century, English dark-coloured serving-bottles may well have borne labels, hence the old term bottle-ticket. In fact, as late as 1740, Dean Swift mentions in his will 'some enamelled silver plates to distinguish bottles of wine by'. The wine label, as we know it, dates from the first half of the eighteenth century, and was used, for the most part, as a pendant to the necks of clear glass decanters, but was, nevertheless, often still referred to as a bottle-ticket. As with stamps, it is surprising how so small an object can exhibit so much style; for example, a wine label often appears completely out of place on a decanter of a different period.

The general silver collector used to be somewhat high-minded about the mere wine label collector, thinking, unfairly, of him as someone who searched for the lightest possible pieces of hallmarked silver, and paid a token price for them.

2 Three unmarked silver wine labels – two Birmingham labels, stamped, pierced and bright-cut, *Garas*, a medicinal liqueur popular circa 1850; *Noyeau* (sic), *Créme de Noyau*, a liqueur from Martinique popular in the 18th and 19th centuries. The *Sherry* perhaps made in the Far East for an English regimental mess.

Nowadays, things have changed, and the price of wine labels has risen considerably, even for those made of other materials such as old Sheffield plate, early examples called 'copper-backs'; enamel on copper; ivory; bone; mother-of-pearl and porcelain (illustration 13).

Collectors' themes

There are many possible themes for wine label collectors who, by concentrating on a particular aspect, may limit expenditure and thus be in a better position to afford the prize piece when it appears. The collector may trace fashions in wines by correlating the relative numbers of different labels produced in different decades, be it the ubiquitous Port or Sherry or the, nowadays, almost forgotten

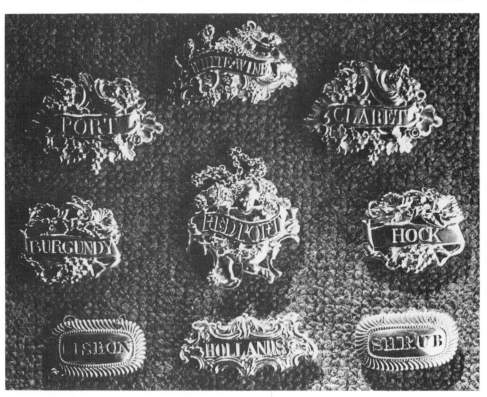

3   Cast silver labels spanning a hundred years
Top middle, Sandylands Drinkwater, 2nd mark
Top left and right, John Harvey, 1745
Middle row, All unmarked; centre label? Keene, Dublin 1790
Bottom row left to right, John Reiley, London 1822? Saml. Whitford, 1866, Charles Rawlings, no date

wines like Bucellas and Mountain. He can specialise in rare titles and it is surprising how many of these exist, often oddly spelt, almost as if different manufacturers vied with each other to produce out-of-the-way names; perhaps they made them to satisfy a contemporary one-up-manship in the choice of wines. Single wine names can be collected in a variety of spellings, such as Madeira, which has at least nine different variants. In this particular case, however, one would eventually be confronted with the dilemma of whether or not to include Malmsey and rarities like Bual, Sercial, Terrantez, as yet unrecorded, and Verdelho. Wine labels from the colonies would form an

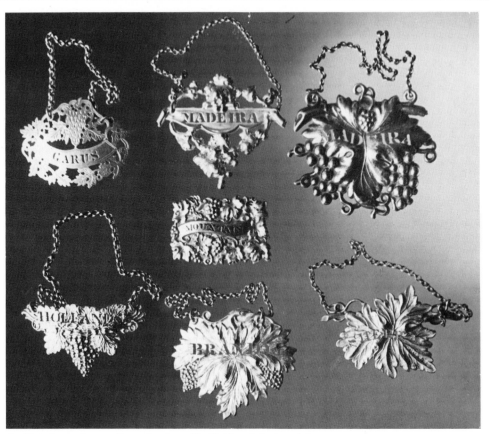

4 The vine and grape theme in silver, Sheffield and electro-plate

unusual group and it is still possible to procure nineteenth century examples of Indian boars' tusks and tigers' claws, mounted in silver, as decorative labels. There are four rare Australian examples, in the collection of the Goldsmiths' Company, by Alexander Dick, a free settler who, in spite of being transported to Norfolk Island for receiving, made the only recorded pre-1850 silver wine labels in Australia.

The collector has the choice of specialising in cast, stamped or wrought silver; he may go in for Irish, Scottish, or other provincial hallmarks; confine himself to one or two makers, whether male or female, or prefer commemorative or armorial examples. Shapes may take his fancy and the choice is wide, be it crescents, escutcheons, scrolls, rectangles, single letters, shells, or vine leaves (illustration 4).

Silver labels

5   An Australian label, by courtesy of the Goldsmiths' Company

Apart from the list of hallmarks from Goldsmiths' Hall, Gutter Lane, the first step for the tyro is to acquire the little sheets of makers' marks from the Wine Label Circle and two inexpensive booklets; *Wine Labels,* by the Circle's honorary secretary, the Reverend E. W. Whitworth, 1966, and *Bottle Tickets*, HMSO, second impression, 1964. Armed with these necessary aids he can make good progress, looking more closely at the subject of his choice.

There was no legal obligation to hallmark wine labels until an act of 1790 concerning the marking of silver plate. Prior to that, some hallmarking of small silver articles, including wine labels, was done occasionally on a voluntary basis. Usually, however, the marking was incomplete and often the pieces were struck only with the maker's initials. Unfortunately, some of the earliest labels have no marks at all, especially, the group of desirable early escutcheons, dating, perhaps, from about 1730, which are shaped with an almost rectangular outline and, at best, boldly engraved in script lettering. Few of these rarities survive: only one, *Vidonia*, in Roman capitals not script, is illustrated in Penzer's *The Book of the Wine Label*, 1974, but none in *Wine, Spirit and Sauce Label*, by Herbert C. Dent, 1933. One of this group, *White Wine* is in the Weed Collection, New York; a *Lisbon* and a *Cyder*, in script, and a *Malt*, in capitals, can be seen at the Victoria and Albert Museum, and there is a *Claret* in script from the Reverend E. W. Whitworth's collection and an *Ale* in capitals, of slightly different shape, in the Sandeman Collection. Another *Claret*, in the Victoria and Albert Museum (M 508–1944), has the letters carefully cut out and there is some additional, engraved decoration in a restrained early style. The essential simplicity of their design recently led a famous London silver dealer to let me purchase my one prized example for a comparatively small sum; he considered it to be late eighteenth century, the unmarked attempt of an amateur of little consequence. Who is to say which of us is correct, especially as there is a script *Whiskey* of the same shape by Phipps and Robinson (1795) in the Sandeman collection which, of course, I suspect is either a refurbishment with re-engraving or a replacement? Indeed, Phipps and Robinson were not the only makers who sometimes reproduced earlier designs, apparently to complete a set.

Better known are the shield-shaped escutcheons of the 1730s to the 1750s made, for example, by Sandylands Drinkwater, Lewis Hamon, John Harvey, and Edward Medlycott; some of them are attractively chased with a tracery of grapes and vine leaves. (Illustration 16 shows four examples.) Cast labels by

6   Unmarked

Sandylands Drinkwater are notable for fine workmanship especially those with the Bacchanalian design known, somewhat inappropriately as *Two Cupids* (top of illustration 3). This design was produced by different makers over a period of about two hundred years. A desirable item could be one of these labels bearing Drinkwater's 1735 mark and perhaps even the pre-1739 variant of the Lion hallmark.

Leading wine merchants usually give extremely good value at the least expensive end of their list, and, indeed, they can scarcely afford to do otherwise and protect their good name. Somewhat in the same way, there is real quality to be found in wine labels made by famous silversmiths such as Hester Bateman, registered 1761, Matthew Boulton and John Fothergill, registered 1773, Paul Storr, registered 1793, Robert Garrard, registered 1802, Benjamin Smith, registered 1807, and E. E. J. & W. Barnard, registered 1828.

Cast labels by the Barnards are a pleasure to handle, especially those crisply moulded with flowers and grapes. Robert Garrard's *Fox and Grapes* is perhaps his most distinctive pattern, and now difficult to acquire. Paul Storr's productions have a monumental quality like commemorative medallions: for example, his heavy silver-gilt *Clover Leaf* design and, in keeping with the rites of Bacchus, the fine relief depicting *Grapes Vines and a Panther Pelt*. The less ambitious Boulton and Fothergill design of *Festooned Drapery*, dated as early as 1774, was also made by that firm in fine quality Sheffield plate.

Nowadays, the silver of well-known and respected plate workers, such as the foregoing, tends to command a very high price, and this is true even for their wine labels; so much so that the average collector is unlikely to find many in this category that he can afford. He may, however, turn elsewhere and fancy the style of less renowned ladies than Hester Bateman, say for example Elizabeth Morley, registered 1794, Susanna Barker, registered 1778, or my own particular favourite, Margaret Binley, registered 1764. If a Matthew Boulton is unobtainable, there are the other Birmingham makers to search for and find, such as George Unite, registered 1844, a man with a somewhat uneven output as regards quality (see illustration 8, third in top row), Joseph Willmore, registered 1820, or Matthew Linwood, registered 1812. Many Birmingham labels were die-stamped, or cut-out for cheapness and speed of manufacture; they often exhibit a peculiar flatness which is relieved, to some extent, by bright-cutting (see illustration 2).

Early in a collector's career, he may well find some of the fine quality work from the more prolific firms of the late eighteenth and early nineteenth centuries (see illustration 9), including Phipps and Robinson, registered 1783, John Reiley,

7   A Paul Storr label, 1810, by courtesy of the Goldsmiths' Company

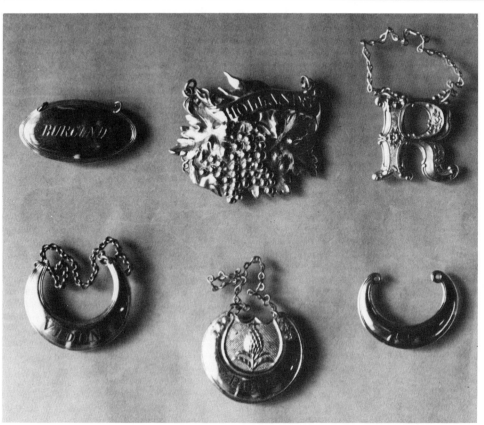

8 R for rum, by George Unite, 1846; the others, Sheffield and electro-plate

registered 1801, Charles Rawlings, registered 1817, Mary and Charles Reiley, registered 1826, Rawlings and Summers, and Reiley and Storer, both registered 1829. Labels by these makers are likely to be the only ones still available in any number, and they may provide a last chance for the would-be collector to concentrate on a particular theme. It is remarkable that where a collection has been carefully selected within certain imposed limits, the whole reflects the personality of the collector and by so doing takes on a special interest and an added value. In a few years it will be too late to form any sizeable collection of early labels, since the choice is rapidly diminishing and the price rising. One should, undoubtedly, buy when the opportunity occurs, remembering that,

9 Die-stamped labels by London makers, 1820s to 1830s
Top and lower left, Mary and Charles Reiley, 1827
Top right, Charles Reiley and George Storer, 1839
Bottom right Reiley and Storer, 1832/3

10 Bat label, by courtesy of
Sotheby's

even at today's prices, a well-formed collection will, in years to come, prove to be a valuable asset, besides providing considerable interest and pleasure over the long term.

There are those veteran collectors who specialise in a particular period, collecting only labels in the Rococo style, say from 1727, the Adam, from 1765, Regency, from 1810, or the Victorian style from 1837 (see illustrations 4, 8 and 12). Others, with a more general outlook, may even include some modern

10 Top to bottom, unmarked; Samuel Davenport, London, 1823; ditto; John Lawrence & Co., B'ham, 1825/6; John Wren, London, 1800/1

examples; however, I have yet to hear of anyone brave enough to confine his collecting solely to the latter. To tempt anyone likely to be converted to this approach, there are some fine present-day wine labels, made by silversmiths such as Frank Clark and Michael Driver, which are by no means just replicas of previous patterns. Then there are modern commemorative labels for which the Wine Label Circle has been responsible for three in the past thirty years: in particular, the fifty-six Elizabeth II Coronation examples by Crichton Brothers, 1952/53, and the more recent label cast by William Egan and Sons of Cork, in an edition of only thirty-five, which resembles the Gleninsheen collar and bears the Irish EEC commemorative mark for 1973. A unique assemblage of modern silver labels, some perhaps especially commissioned, could well prove to be very rewarding in the future, if one may judge by the remarkably high price of several hundred pounds apiece in a recent sale for a set of six cast and extensively hand-worked nineteenth century examples depicting a large bat with wings fully extended, a design which most of us have always considered to be frankly ugly. Nevertherless, these large bat labels are rather mysterious, as they are always unmarked and, apart from this set of six, comprising *Claret, Brandy, Madeira, Port, Sherry* and *Whisky*, there are few other such sets known. It has been suggested that bat labels, of which there are various sizes and qualities, were not made in Europe, but perhaps in India. When writing this article, I happened to discover that in 1883 there were three British registered designs of bats with wings extended and one of these was for silver, probably a wine label. This design is by James Barclay Hennell, 1828–1899, a London silversmith who is well known for his representations of animals and whose famous brother, Robert, 1826–1892, was responsible for some good quality labels. The Mammal Section of the British Museum, however, considers that our bat could be a stylized portrayal of the Indian dog-faced fruit bat, *Cynopterus sphinx*. This makes the Indian origin of these labels more likely.

Sheffield plate

Although there are numerous, often quite modern, die-stamped and electro-plated labels (illustration 12), there are comparatively few early Sheffield plate examples on the market, especially the earliest escutcheons called 'copper-backs'. In the south of England, at any rate, the silver counterparts are more easily found. Many of the earliest Sheffield plate labels, like the attractive and varied snuff boxes in the same material, were probably produced in Birmingham in the second half of the eighteenth century, some time before Matthew Boulton of that city made his Adam-style design of *Festooned Drapery*, in silver and plate.

12 Electro-plate labels showing a wide range of design from the Victorian period onwards

Tusk

Splayed neck rings of varying size cut from elephant tusks date mostly from the early nineteenth century, there being no reason to date them any earlier than the majority of silver examples. *Bucellas* (illustration 13) is one of the commonest names on these collars and the champagne *Ay Mousseux*, in the Cropper

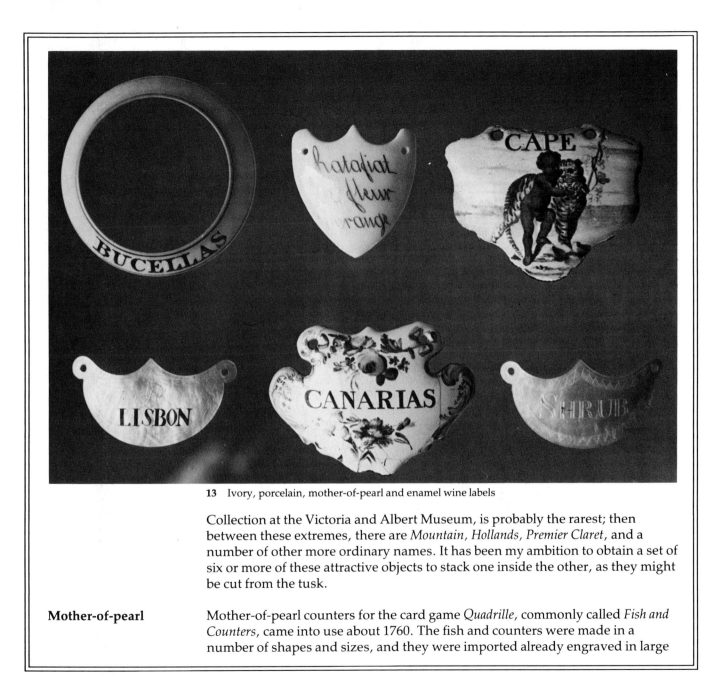

13 Ivory, porcelain, mother-of-pearl and enamel wine labels

Collection at the Victoria and Albert Museum, is probably the rarest; then between these extremes, there are *Mountain, Hollands, Premier Claret*, and a number of other more ordinary names. It has been my ambition to obtain a set of six or more of these attractive objects to stack one inside the other, as they might be cut from the tusk.

Mother-of-pearl   Mother-of-pearl counters for the card game *Quadrille*, commonly called *Fish and Counters*, came into use about 1760. The fish and counters were made in a number of shapes and sizes, and they were imported already engraved in large quantities from China: '*Morning Post*, 6 December, 1775, To be sold by the proprietor of a China Shop, lately arrived from China, Quadrille Pools, Fish and Counters'. Examination of mother-of-pearl wine labels suggests that some of my own examples at any rate, are also Chinese in origin, showing the same style of engraving and the same patterns as on the Quadrille counters. Some of the fish and counters were even adapted as wine labels and engraved, possibly in England, with the appropriate names on their sides. There are doubtless a few mother-of-pearl labels, which like some counters, are engraved with crests or coats of arms; these could prove to be a newly discovered branch of Chinese export armorial wares.

Porcelain

Penzer has a page of porcelain labels which look like memorial tablets from a French cemetery; indeed the majority of these labels appear to be French of the nineteenth century and to have little artistic merit. The most aesthetically satisfactory ones are not illustrated by Penzer; they are made of high-fired, greyish porcelain produced at Bayeux. Shaped as a small shield less than $1\frac{3}{4}$ inches wide they are inscribed in gold script lettering with such titles as *Vergus* and *Ratafiat de Fleur d'Orange* (illustration 13).

Enamel

Penzer's enamel labels are even less attractive than his porcelain selection, in fact it would be difficult to find another assorted group of fourteen labels to demonstrate more clearly what not to collect in the way of fakes and modern reproductions. Almost invariably, it seems, when a silver wine label collector writes about enamels he chooses 'wrong ones' to illustrate, and these are usually nineteenth century French reproductions.

The porcelain and enamel productions of the Samson Factory in Paris have bedevilled collectors since they were first made in 1845. The factory was founded by Emile Samson at Montreuil Sous Bois and still exists today, although under new management for the last twenty five years or so. Their present trade card reads *Reproduction Exacte de Pièces Anciennes*; this description used to include hard-paste copies of eighteenth century porcelain, mostly figures, and enamel copies of eighteenth century snuff boxes, caskets, and wine labels. A number of their labels, for example an *Eau de Lubin*, have 'Dreyfous 99 Mount St. W'. in fired black enamel on the reverse. When I visited the factory recently, I found and photographed a drawer full of enamel labels; entirely old stock, as they are no longer made.

Eighteenth century enamel labels were mostly manufactured in Birmingham, and later, perhaps, in south Staffordshire; they are pretty things decorated with

14 A Samson enamel wine label

15 Birmingham enamel circa 1775

hand-painted floral designs. In a different class, however, are the sensitive transfer-prints of *putti* from designs by James Gwin on the distinctive escutcheon-shaped Battersea labels, 1753 to 1756 (see illustrations 1 and 13, third in top row). The engraver John Brooks seems to have been responsible for the printing side of the business at Battersea, using a process he claimed to have invented two years previously in Birmingham. Simon François Ravenet engraved the copper plates from these designs, and his remarkable depth of line can only be fully appreciated where there is no over-painting, although the labels were sold from the factory, both 'colour'd and uncolour'd'. Battersea labels exhibit two variants of the escutcheon shape on which over forty different titles are now recorded and over twenty different designs, all of them now both rare and costly. Because of the short period of production they give important information about the wine imported at that comparatively early date; *Cape* and *Moselle*, for example, occur here much earlier than on silver labels. *Morache* and *Mulseau* are two extreme rarities that have only recently come to light.

Apart from the Battersea prints and a small group of large escutcheons transfer-printed in black which are close copies, though in reverse, of the Battersea designs, there are no other known transfer-printed enamel labels. The Birmingham and south Staffordshire labels are painted with scrolls, floral sprays, swags, and bunches of grapes (see illustration 13, middle of second row); and except for the occasional ribbons and festooned drapery, there is comparatively little variation, and there are no pictorial designs. The different shapes of escutcheons are of interest as they are unlike any known silver examples, and only one early type comes anywhere near the Battersea. Altogether there are nine or ten different shapes known to me, some occurring in two sizes.

The painted motives can be matched with those on snuff boxes and the like, and also on Chelsea, and Chelsea-Derby china. The earliest flower sprigs are comparable with those painted in the 'red anchor' period, 1753 to 1758, and one hand, in particular, closely resembles that found on a 1755-dated enamel snuff box in the Victoria and Albert Museum (C 118–1963). Another artist produced more tightly drawn and stylised designs, placing little accents at the tips of leaves and petals to give them life, a mannerism that was continued into the 1780's. A freer style of painting matches that seen in the reserves on Staffordshire *étuis*, with their coloured grounds, raised gilding and portraits of ladies from contemporary mezzotints, the equivalent, in Chelsea, of the 'gold anchor-marked' period, about 1758 to 1769. The majority of labels, however, seem to be later still, and to parallel the Chelsea-Derby style of painting

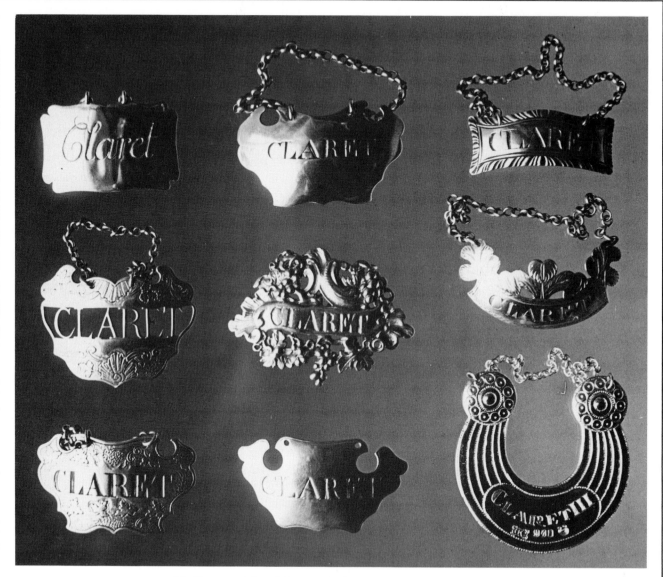

16 Top row, right to left, unmarked; Walter Brind, London, entered 1857; John Harvey, ent. 1737.
Middle row, Richard Binley, no date; John Harvey, 1745 mark; 'W J & Co', no date.
Bottom row, Sandylands Drinkwater, 2nd mark; ?Samuel Teare, Dublin; W. Egan, Cork, 1973

112

1770-1784; the chief ornament is usually a hanging swag centred on a pink rose. Judging from silver labels, it was during this time that a much greater variety of wines was imported and this is mirrored in the titles of these labels, many of which are rare names such as *Coulanges, Avalon,* and *Tonnerre*.

Finally some large deeply-indented escutcheons are painted in rather matt colours and these, although continuing an early shape, seem to be dated from the last quarter of the eighteenth century. The titles have now reverted to being more commonplace, typically *Claret, Sherry, Port* and *Rum* but also various liqueurs: *Chartreuse, Crème de Menthe* and *Curaçao*.

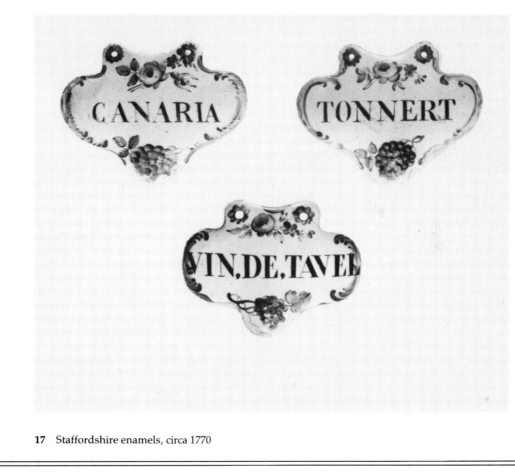

17   Staffordshire enamels, circa 1770

113

The winery

The 'fermentary'

Lake's Folly *Max Lake*

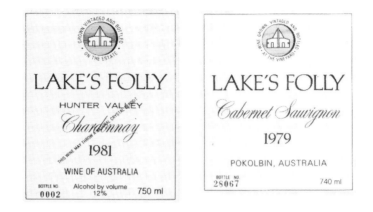

We begin with the soil

As an established surgeon, and something of a wine buff, I tasted, in 1960, a 1930 Hunter red, half each *cabernet-sauvignon* and *petit verdot,* made 100 miles from where I then lived in Sydney. It was the best wine I had tasted up to that time. I was moved to 'have a go' and I dug holes in all sorts of soil profiles for three years. It helps in a way, if you are starting the first new family vineyard in living memory; you're first in and can get the best selection, even if there is no one to talk to. Wind, hail and rain patterns were studied and grape growing and wine making were closely observed.

There have been three seas over the Hunter River catchment in geological aeons. Soils in the area vary greatly, more so at the Folly. The red grape plantings run east-west, contoured to some degree, on the cooler south-east segment of a lime-rich volcanic hill. Ploughed chunks quickly weather and fret to a granular texture which is ideal for good drainage, the *sine qua non* of good grape growing. An alluvial silted creek-flat bears most of the *chardonnay,* with rather heavy yellow clay deeper down. We took the trouble to deep-rip this, filling the cross hatchings of the upper tines with light stuff in which the vines were planted.

All the soil details that once seemed so important are seen somewhat differently. The intrinsic relation of the dirt and the adjoining micro-climate loom larger now. For example, the solar reflection from light-coloured soil on gravel may even be critical where temperature could render grape quality marginal, apart from the influence on soil texture and drainage.

<table>
<tr><td>Varieties</td><td>

The plan was to get something like the Bordeaux mix. It took some years to realise that this varied considerably in different years even from the same *château*. So we now have about 30 acres under vine, about 16 *cabernet-sauvignon*, and the rest of the red mainly *hermitage (shiraz)* which latter has made fine reds at Pokolbin for more than a century. There is a little *malbec*, a spoonful of *merlot* (which does not do well at Lake's Folly) and this year a small trial of *petit verdot* has been commenced; only recently available in Australia, I remember it from the 1930 vintage that lit the fire under me.

Deterred by the expense of French champagne, in 1969 the first small *chardonnay* plot was begun. They almost all died, our only unsuccessful planting ever. Lake's luck though, they turned out to have been *pinot blanc*. Next year we got the right stuff. The idea of making a *blanc de blancs* was abandoned when clients started raving about the 1974 base wine, and offered rewards to keep it that way, rather than *champenoise* it. Serendipity again. There are now nearly ten acres bearing.

In 1963 nothing was known in Australia of the production improvements possible with clonal selection; we made do just with cuttings off beautiful old vines whose lineage traced back to the first cuttings brought to Australia by James Busby early last century. These may well be part of the appeal of the Folly reds, low production vines that they are.

Many vineyards make a presentable Cabernet from two-to-four year-old vines. The trick is to sustain and improve as the years and foliage gather. Marvellous to relate, this is indeed happening under Stephen Lake's direction.

</td></tr>
</table>

The Hunter Valley climate

Great achievements need great efforts to overcome great climatic difficulties. The making of great wine is a case in point. Where it is easy to grow, the vine seldom produces really great wine. Climate has always been the major Hunter Valley problem, where the making of wine must be one of the severest challenges to man by nature, and vice-versa.

The bare record of local temperature suggests the sub-tropics where no consulting oenologist in his right mind would advise anyone to plant today, were it not already so renowned for the intensity of flavour and lightness of body of its wines. Twenty or so miles inland, the almost daily cloud cover has been suggested as the ameliorating factor that approaches the micro-climates of

Bordeaux and Burgundy. Humidity can be severe, with downy mildew a fact of life, controlled by routine use of copper and similar sprays during the growing season. What we cannot control are the Coral Sea cyclones, Fred and Mavis and the like, which strike the Queensland coast and funnel down the Great Dividing Range to Pokolbin, 1,000 miles south, delivering unwelcome torrents during the vintage in February and March. We must be the only primary industry in Australia that does not mind drought, at that season, anyhow.

A major and totally unexpected setback has now passed, for the present at least. Alcan established an aluminium smelter at Kurri Kurri just north of the best vineyards, and this has emitted damaging quantities of highly toxic fluoride for more than a decade. This has only just been properly controlled, and fruit yield and quality have returned to normal. Vineyards in the region faced total annihilation by the establishment of a second smelter nearby by BHP, Australia's biggest company. This extraordinary irresponsibility was encouraged by the New South Wales government. At the eleventh hour the vineyards were reprieved by the downturn in aluminium demand and the rise in energy costs. and perhaps 10,000 local wine-related jobs were saved.

Wine making

The actual making of the wine has been the least of the problems. Any doctor will know what I mean. The medical course starts with botany, introduction to the understanding of natural cycles, fertilisation, cloning, growth, photosynthesis, fruition and harvest, then dormancy – the wheel of life in the making of wine. Then comes biochemistry and the fundamental energy exchange of the Kreks cycle – the vine, the grape, the yeast, the maker and the taster, all of us happily metabolising to such great purpose nitrogen, vitamins, the lot. Bacteriology, public health and so many other disciplines add to wine making. If you have worked through the night at the bedside of a very ill patient you acquire the sensitivity to the biological variation needed to make great wine. Indeed!

And how diligently we at the Folly continue to work at the marriage of art and technology, with traditional open fermentation of reds, but with highly-bred yeasts and fine temperature control.

The winery

The master plan was drawn on the back of a cigarette carton in 1962. Non-smokers now, we need proper drawing paper. The building has certainly attracted attention with a functional impact akin to Paris's Pompidou Centre, but years before the latter, of course. Visitors look around the upper storey accommodation, and occasionally ask when we propose to finish it. On the other hand, architects ask many more questions. The first stage (1964) has a profile which has become the Folly logo – an A-frame of mahogany telephone poles. The bush carpentry was really cheap at the time, less so when trying to marry the wooden irregularities to the steel additions of the north and south wings in 1970 and 1977. It now houses the fermentary, two years' volume of large and small cooperage for reds, and a cool small barrel room for the Chardonnay. In the family and guest wing there is a rather startling horseshoe table that can seat 40, though not in any opulence. There is also a cellar *oenothèque*.

The Lake family

From the family viewpoint it looked like a break even situation for some years. Any wife supporting her husband in the years of establishment and difficulty has every right to ponder the lack of overseas travel and other touches of luxury so long delayed. My marvellous wife, Joy, was reared in very difficult wheat and sheep country. A medical husband seemed insurance against repetition of those fearful childhood cycles of drought, fire and flood, till one morning, in her words, she woke 'next to a grape cocky' (battling farmer).

Her other fear, that the vineyard would divide the family, was less substantiated. They all hopped in, helping with might and main. Now our youngest son, Stephen, is setting his own fine stamp on the Folly style, with the reputation of the wines waxing yearly. All credit to him, it is more demanding to hone and polish after the lessening of the momentum of the early creative flush. Lake's Folly is the only vineyard to achieve top rating in both reds and whites in each edition of Robin Bradley's *Australian Wine Vintages*.

It is given to few so richly to fulfil their dream. Talent, energy and willing help from family, friends and neighbours synergise. Even disaster and disappointment can convert or give new direction. It helps to be 'fortune's child'. It may well be that starting a vineyard and making good wine really indicate the philosophical tuning of a lifestyle.

Unsolicited testimonals

The '68 and '69 Lake Folly Cabernet Sauvignon: 'The wines are in top world class; anyone who tastes the wines for the first time will look at Australia in a new light.' David Peppercorn (1979) perhaps has been too kind, but there is no doubt that the wines and vineyard have caught the attention of the connoisseurs worldwide.

'One of the important vineyards of the world', in the view of Robin Bradley (1982), who also described 'the ultimate Hunter River Cabernet, with truffled overtones of the best of Pomerol'.

Michael Broadbent (1980), about the '76 Chardonnay tasted in 1977: 'lovely yellow colour, fine bouquet, medium dryness and body, fabulously expanding rich flavour, smoky, arguably the best Australian Chardonnay,'

Recommended reading

Bradley, Robin The Small Wineries of Australia (Macmillan, Melbourne, 1982)

Broadbent, Michael The Great Vintage Wine Book (Mitchell Beazley, London, 1980)

Lake, David Lake's Folly. ('Notes from the Winery Floor' in The Australian Wine Browser, Ed. Anders Ousback; David Ell Press, Sydney, 1979)

Lake, Max Hunter Winemakers (Jacaranda Press, Brisbane, 1970)

Peppercorn, David et al. Drinking Wine (Macdonald, London, 1979)

Verulam, Bussaco and Burg Windeck *Michael Broadbent*, MW

Verulam is the title of an English family, taken from the name of the Roman town on the outskirts of the ancient city of St Albans in Hertfordshire; Bussaco, or Buçaco, is the name of a former royal hunting lodge and an hotel, set in high forests in the middle of Portugal; Burg Windeck a lofty castle in Baden, with one of Germany's few two-rosette restaurants at its foot. How are the three connected? I shall try to explain.

The train of thought was started by a chance remark made by Heinrick Wehlauer the chef/proprietor of the Burg Windeck at the end of the longest and most memorable food-and-wine occasion of my life. It was last May. Below the balcony of the restaurant were impossibly steep slopes of vines from which, Herr Wehlauer told me, he gathered grapes to make a wine which had more than local renown but which he refused to sell, except in his restaurant. Not great he said, for the vineyard was really too high, but unique and, with his cooking and the spectacular view across the broad Rhine valley towards the Vosges and Haardt ranges, one of the several attractions of the establishments (I would number at least one of his waitresses amongst the others.)

The situation reminded me of another spectacular hotel/restaurant in a not dissimilar high forest setting that I had had a great urge to visit, and have an even greater one to return to. For at Bussaco they make, in a delightfully old-fashioned way, one of the least-known but most characterful wines of the world. You have to *go* there to drink it.

Tommy Layton

But where does Verulam come in? Well this is a little story which takes me back to my first year in the wine trade. It was in the early 1950s and I was a trainee with one of that dying breed, a true English eccentric, Tommy Layton. TAL wrote assiduously. One of his many endearing traits was the way he could tell jokes against himself and, by doing so, make clearly painful experiences, for him and for others, into delightful episodes. He ran a wine restaurant – which is perhaps as well, for on £300 a year I would have starved had it not been for my friendly relationship with the irascible Irish cook, Molly; a wine bar, run by a sweeter-natured Irish girl, Brigit, and a wine business (I was the chap who typed, packed and delivered the orders). But probably the greatest influence on my life, though I don't think I realised it at the time, was his wine tasting group, The Circle of Wine Tasters. Tommy's tastings were enormously varied and imaginative, and the members were, as I recall, delightful. One was John Grimston, a Member of Parliament and, as I was to learn later, an avid wine collector. His brother was the 5th Earl of Verulam and their shared cellar was of the classic English shape and size, beneath the stone flagged 40-foot-cube hall of the family seat, Gorhambury.

Gorhambury

Well, a wine treasure hunt was to be arranged for the Circle at Gorhambury. I drove Tommy up the A6 in his splendid, open, green label Bentley – which is a story in itself. I had never driven an old vintage car before; indeed my father was also something of an eccentric too, but in an opposite way to TAL, for he would never allow me to drive any of his cars. Tommy to my amazement, not only asked me to drive his magnificent machine but – and this was to become a worrying responsibility – merely handed me the keys, sketched the dashboard instruments and calmly told me to collect it from a cramped car park beneath a modern block of flats near Baker Street. It didn't take me long to start the engine, but it took me ages to manoeuvre it out of the garage. Then, for some 40 minutes, I drove it round and round Regent's Park to get used to double-declutching. Eventually, I arrived in Manchester Square, the rich throbbing of the engine causing all windows to be opened out of curiosity, or closed to avoid the noise. A bit like Concorde . . .

Anyway, we arrived at Gorhambury, drawing up under a magnificent portico. I remember cricket was being played on the lawn in front. Then we got down to planning the treasure hunt. All done, we assembled in the morning room for drinks and for what I imagined was a light snack. Having had my fill, but persuaded by Mrs Grimston to finish the last sandwich, I was somewhat mortified when the butler – as in a West End play – gracefully opened the double doors and made that classic announcement 'My lord, luncheon is served'. Brushing an evasive piece of cress from my mouth, I sheepishly followed the party downstairs. And, since I was young, hungry and impressionable at that period of my life, seated next to his Lordship I dutifully despatched a many-course lunch.

Some 25 years later I received a telephone call. It was the Earl of Verulam. Would I visit Gorhambury to value the cellar? I drove down, a little nostalgically. No cricket on the lawn that day, but a pleasant young man on a farm tractor greeted me. He turned out to be the present incumbent. John Grimston had inherited the title and estate from his elder brother, and this was John's son.

The cellar was full of treasures. Not just good burgundy and old claret, but venerable Tokay and a collection of weird and wonderful wines. The bin which really baffled me contained several vintages of wine labelled Buçaco Tinto. I had never heard of Buçaco but it looked interesting so, with some difficulty, I eventually found reference to the place in an old guide book. Out of curiosity we tried a couple of lots in a Christie Fine Wine Sale. I couldn't resist buying a bottle myself, and from that moment on I had a consuming passion to visit the place.

Bussaco

The opportunity arose in the autumn of 1979 when I was invited to be guest speaker at the annual treasurer's (chairman's) dinner at the Factory House in Oporto. My wife and I managed to squeeze in a weekend at Bussaco the weekend prior so I could relax and prepare my speech. A hair-raising journey – Portuguese drivers match their roads – two or three hours drive south from Oporto brought us to a steep spiralling drive up to one of the most extraordinary buildings I have ever seen in my life. It had been a royal hunting lodge-cum-grand hotel, a heavily ornate mansion in the Portuguese rococo style known as Manueline. It seemed to me a mixture of Victorian gothic and Disneyworld with a dash of mad King Ludwig of Bavaria; a monumental pile of elaborately carved white stone, nestling in one of the great mountain forests of Europe. Hugh Johnson, as great an expert on matters arboreal as on wine, tells me that the variety of trees is almost without parallel, and one species grows there which thrives nowhere else in the world.

Despite the recent revolution in Portugal, clearly nothing had changed. The property has long been owned by the state but leased, for almost as long, to the d'Almeida family. Inside, the atmosphere reminded me a little of the grand

The Palace Hotel, Bussaco

hotels of Buxton or Harrogate in their heyday. Many more staff than guests, all charming, and a manager José Rodrigues dos Santos (I have his card stuck into my tasting book) who, when I asked him – later – how long he had been at Bussaco, said, with a wry smile, 'too long': since 1934!

Lunch in the cellar

Happily, Mr Rodrigues was not merely keen on wine, it was his consuming passion. Moreover, he took an interest in the vineyards and was responsible for the wine making. He told me he spends most of the autumn in the cellars and, to get away from the guests in the season, he disappears downstairs every Saturday afternoon to cook local sausages in brandy washed down with a fresh young vintage. We were there on a Saturday and he kindly asked us to join him.

Of the 21 vintages of red Buçaco on the list, the youngest (this was in 1979 remember) was 1974, and the oldest, by a happy coincidence, my own birth year, 1927. So I had no hesitation in choosing this as our main wine for dinner that night.

There were 17 vintages of Buçaco Branco (it is spelt Bussaco in the brochures and Buçaco on the labels), from '74 back to halves of the '28. I chose, out of curiosity, the '34 for dinner on Sunday, being advised to try the '44 before the '27 red on the Saturday night.

The hard work of selecting wines for two dinners being over, we settled down at a small table in the middle of the cellar to share Mr Rodrigues's mid-afternoon treat: large local sausages cooked in Aguardente Buçaco, the Reserva Especial no less, in a rough earthenware bowl and washed down with a bottle of the '58 tinto. Our cook/*maître de chai*/manager meanwhile told us about Bussaco.

The story of Bussaco The head of the Order of Carmelites discovered this virgin forest and, in 1629, a monk skilled in masonry came with five brothers to select a site for the new monastery, part way down the hillside, 'on the greenest slope, open to the fresh sea air, yet sheltered by high rocks'. The following year the community moved in. The Carmelites vowed to plant, every year, more trees to enrich their land and, in addition to native maples, laurels and oaks, planted newly imported trees like the Mexican cypress. In 1689 Louis XIV's botanist came to Bussaco and counted 42 different kinds. Happily, despite the disbanding of religious orders in Portugal in the early 19th century, tree planting continued: the monkey puzzle from New Zealand, cedar from the Himalayas, white ash from America, camphor from Japan, acacia and gumtree from Australia. Bussaco became one of the finest botanical museums in the world.

But how did the monastery become a royal hunting lodge? Sometime after the dissolution, various members of the Portuguese royal family used to visit the forest. They felt it an ideal place for a hunting lodge and eventually King Carlos, encouraged by his minister of public works, agreed that it would be a suitable and healthy place for royal holidays. They then had the idea of creating a big modern hotel of the sort Portuguese travellers had seen on the French riviera, with a private wing for royal use. It would be a true 'palace' hotel, crowned with a tower to overlook the highest tree tops.

An Italian architect, the finest masons, and a bevy of Portuguese artists to decorate the interior, took 11 years to complete the hotel which was finally opened in 1909. Unhappily, King Carlos never set foot in it: he was assassinated in February 1908, and his son Manuel II reigned only long enough to spend one holiday there, in 1910, his last on Portuguese soil. But Bussaco became fashionable. It was, still is, a stone's throw from Luso, a sporting spa. In 1920 Alexandre d'Almeida, a native of Luso, moved up to manage and develop the hotel, building up its reputation for country food and fine local wine. It hasn't changed.

A page from the author's tasting book, with a sketch of the cellars and the brandy label

As a footnote for English lovers of history, it was in the monastery at Bussaco that Wellington slept before the battle in 1810 which was to be the turning point in French fortunes. The *coup de grâce* was finally given to Napoleon's Iberian Peninsula incursion at Torres Vedras. Further north, Wellington's men pushed the French out of Oporto and his officers, billeted there, greatly took to vintage port . . .

Burg Windeck – aperitif and light lunch

Talking of battles, castles weren't built for fun and I suppose that the ruins of Burg Windeck, where I began these reminiscences, must have been the site of some rough times, overlooking as it does, the much fought over Rhine valley. On a less palatial scale, the Wehlauers are doing for the restaurant there just what the d'Almeidas did at Bussaco. But even in their heyday I doubt if the latter had ever provided or witnessed such a feast as that at Burg Windeck on 28 May 1983. I was the guest of Jean Hugel at an annual tasting-cum-lunch of a group of French and German wine lovers.

We limbered up with Krug 1953 in magnums. At 12 noon we sat down to the first course of soup followed by force-fed goose liver with stewed pears, accompanied by Château d'Yquem 1943, 1953 and 1921. Next, lobster with Hugel's '53 Tokay, and turbot on roasted artichoke strips with '63 Wachenheimer Rechbachel Riesling Kabinett of Bürklin-Wolf and a '43 Wehlener Sonnenuhr feinste Auslese of J. J. Prüm. With baby lamb and mushrooms two '59 and two '53 spätburgunders, a '53 Hermitage La Chapelle – corked, the only poor bottle of the day – and '43 La Tâche. Then came pigeon on savoy cabbage accompanied by no less than seven '53 clarets: Beychevelle, lovely, Cos d'Estournel, La Mission-Haut-Brion, Haut-Brion (so much more elegant and suave), Cheval-Blanc, Pétrus, and Lafite (perfection as always). The '59 Lafite was added for fun and then we passed on to six great '53 Moselles: Berncasteler Doktor und Graben hochfeine Auslese of Thanisch, a Wehlen-Zeltinger Sonnenuhr feinste Auslese of J. J. Prüm, a Kanzemer Berg feine Auslese of von Othegraven, and a peach-like Eitelsbacher Karthäuser-Hofberg Burgberg feinste Auslese. Then came a couple of '53 Beerenauslesen: J. J. Prüm's Wehlener Sonnenuhr, with a bouquet like ambrosial lemon curd, on the palate a fresh buttery texture: fabulous, five star. Next the great von Schubert's Maximin Grünhäuser Herrenberg, heavenly nose, ripe peaches, powerful, assertive, drying out a little but years of life. Somewhere in the middle we toyed with finely sliced strawberries in cream, with delicate rhubarb mousse – incredibly delicious.

The grand finale – a fanfare of all that is monumental in German wine –

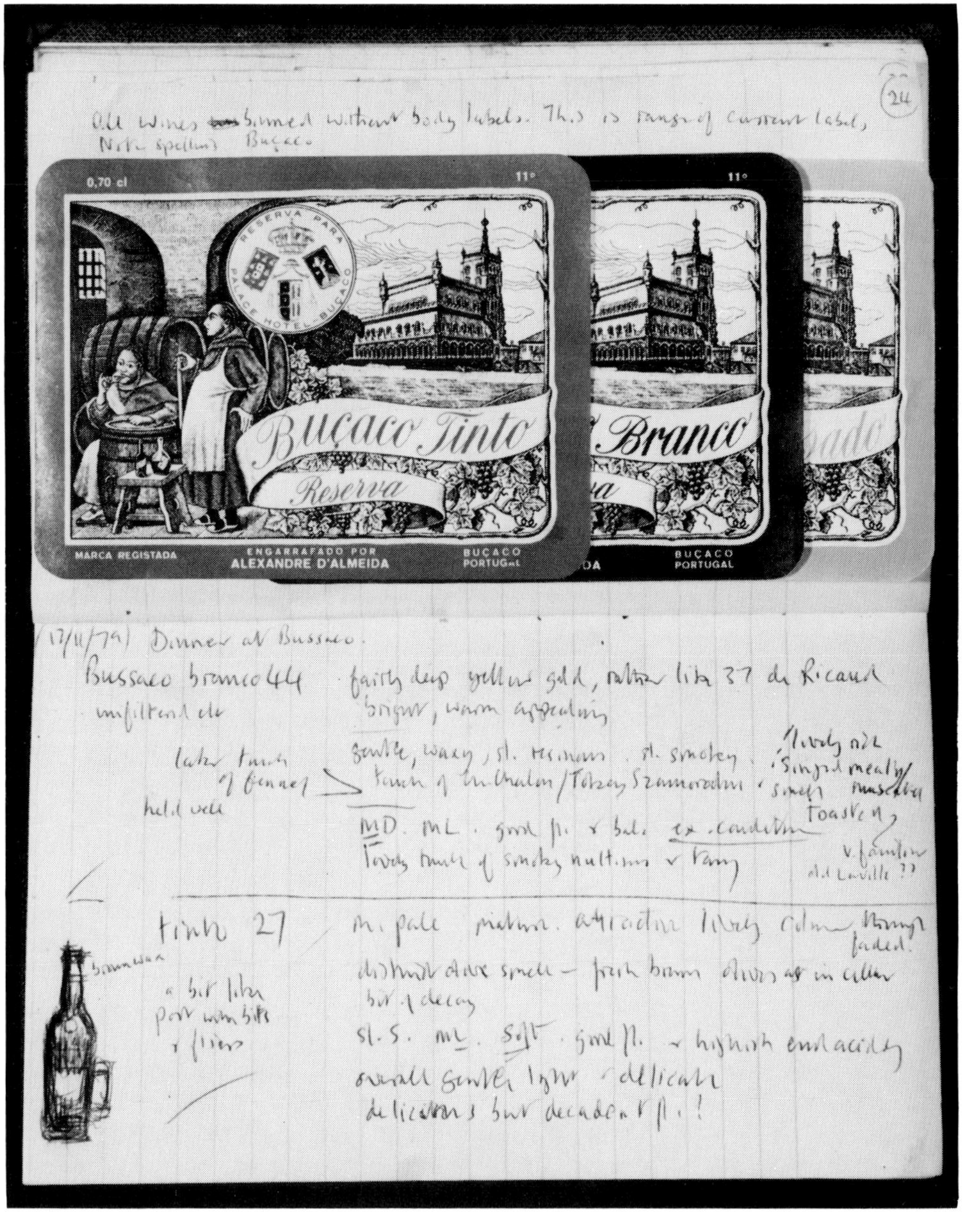

Notes made at Bussaco, with labels.

Burg Windeck

consisted of six trockenbeerenauslesen, all but the first being Rheingaus from the Staatsweingüter, Eltville. These were served with apple flan and cinnamon ice cream.

The first was a great Moselle of a magnificent classic vintage J. J. Prüm's Wehlener-Zeltinger Sonnuhr with a repeat of the lemon curd plus a dash of lime blossom and vanilla on the nose, but beautifully sweet, rich, in fact positively fat on the palate. *Six* stars!

The Rheingau TBAs began with a '37 Rauenthaler Baiken, the deepest of all in colour after the '21 Yquem: a warm amber, almost tawny; a Sauternes-like *crême brulée* bouquet; sweet, full-flavoured, a fresh raisiny style, perfect acidity. Perfection. Next Rauenthaler Pfaffenberg, pale orange-tawny; a deliciously creamy fragrant bouquet; sweet, rich, fabulous flavour, balance and length. Then a '33 Rauenthaler Baiken, one of the palest, and the only one with a slightly mushroomy bouquet; semi-sweet, with a taste of singed raisins. Good acidity but drying out.

The penultimate trockenbeerenauslese was the magnificent '59 Rauenthaler Baiken. Slightly deeper in colour than the '53 Pfaffenberg, a warm rich amber-gold. An amazing bouquet: huge, singed, slightly raisiny, intense. On the palate, sweet and highly concentrated fruit – honey, sultanas – impossible to put into words. Another half century of life. Peter Ziegler, our host, told us that this wine was one of the greats of all time. The over-ripe *edelfaule* grapes had an incredibly high natural sugar content: 248° Oeschle, and 13° of acidity. Almost unheard of.

The last wine of the day was a rare Steinberger Trockenbeerenauslese of Herr Ziegler's birth year, 1943: just a taste, from his last half-bottle. It was intensely yellow, the sort of pure gold of Tutankhamun's mask; a curious, light, delicate bouquet; completely dried out but refreshing and as sound as a bell.

Post prandial

By this time we – there were 20 at the table – all felt somehow exhilarated yet subdued. Not a red nose or fuzzy head amongst us. The English and French party drove back to Riquewihr for a late, simple supper – with a little wine, of course. Despite my notoriously weak head I slept soundly, woke tremendously refreshed and did a couple of quick sketches before breakfast. A quick tour of the cellars, a little tasting – of an 1865 Tokay d'Alsace, one of the few remaining in Hugel's private bin: quite unbelievably perfect, a deep warm amber, honeyed, grapey nose (muscatel and golden syrup), still entrancingly sweet and fat with perfect flavour and acidity, then off to Basle for the flight home.

It all seemed a long way from Manchester, even from Manchester Square . . .

Prospecting for diamonds
Hugo Dunn-Meynell

The line of revellers was just passing the Roosevelt statue in Grosvenor Square when the gentleman wearing a chef's toque suggested that we might all go truffling together some time. You know the sort of ideas the French get on New Year's Eve. The 'chef' really was one – president of the Académie Culinaire in Britain, no less – and we had been discussing truffles shortly before midnight.

It had all started with *les étrennes*, the name the French give to their New Year presents. My own offering had already been consumed, since some liquid was needed to partner the *étrennes* of Emile Jung, patron of Strasbourg's bestarred Restaurant Crocodile – and an appropriate man to lead a conga. He had provided a massive roll of *foie gras*, boldly flecked with black diamonds. This led to reminiscences about Bocuse's *soupe aux truffes en croûte*, the *truffe surprise* of Louis Outhier at La Napoule, the *feuilleté sucré aux truffes* of the Hôtel de France at Auch, and the gloriously vulgar *glace aux truffes* they used to serve at the old Delmonico's in New York. The gently philosophical mood induced by Dom Pérignon had promoted conjecture: how many truffles can a Périgourdin worry down at a sitting? why do pigs so love the smell? do truffles really promote longevity? in what sort of ground do the precious tubers flourish? and (from a lady who had been ambushed under the mistletoe) are truffles really aphrodisiac, or is that the archdeacon's usual style?

I do not know what should be the collective noun for *chefs de cuisine* – an indignation, perhaps? a fricassée? a condiment? a bouillabaisse? But whatever it is assembled three weeks later at Heathrow. There were also a few interlopers, like me and my friend Alec, who sells fish in Billingsgate. And just to give tone to the party, Patrick Forbes who, so far as Dom Pérignon is concerned, 'wrote the book'.

The less said about the journey the better. If Monsieur Viney (formerly of the Ritz) and Monsieur Mouilleron (Ma Cuisine – two knives-and-forks, and a star) can't drink post-phylloxera claret, they could have explained their dietary needs beforehand, just as Alec could have done about the mild-and-bitter. It was, however, short-tempered of the stewardess to suggest that if Mr Edmond (Boodles Club) and Mr Angliss (poulter by appointment to top people) found their champagne too warm, they might like to travel outside. Our leader Michel Bourdin (ex-Maxim's, now of the Connaught) spent much of the flight trying to work out who was missing, and only as the Gironde came into view realised that he was looking for himself.

We were met by a provisioning officer named Rougié, who introduced himself as a member of the *foie gras* trade – indeed, it quickly became evident that he pretty well **is** the *foie gras* trade. He said he would first stop at his farmhouse outside Sarlat for *les amuse-gueule.* At the sound of this, Alec winked broadly at me, but the diversion turned out not to be a turn from the Bal Tabarin. Instead, dish after dish of Monsieur's own heavenly produce was handed round. Better than Montmartre, we decided. We were all telling each other we had not eaten so fine a supper for months when we were led into another room full of the steam of soup made from the famous Périgord pumpkins, *cassoulet de canard sarladais, cabécous* (tiny round goat cheeses), plus a *bombe* flavoured with *eau de noix.* A considerable number of bottles appeared of the rich, dark red wine from Cahors, our destination in Quercy, and last of all a rather splendid walnut liqueur.

The ensuing 150-kilometre cross-country trek was enlivened by Jacques Viney's rousing choruses of *Clementine* with descant by Alec of *Frère Jacques*, which he explained to me is French for scallops. After that, the mock-gothic Hotel Terminus at Cahors was a welcome sight, but I confess I spent little time at 2 am admiring its high slate roof, intricate stained glass and the furnishings and décor unchanged since 1930.

Breakfast bore about as much relationship to a *café complet* at Fouquet's or the Crillon as Yorkshire high tea to cucumber sandwiches at the Ritz. Smoked hams, pâtés, rillettes, salty Roquefort and thinly-veined *fromage bleu de Quercy*; coffee,

Left top, Diane the huntress
Below, Le moment critique
Above, Hans gets the scent

tea, young Cahors wine and Perrier (both in the magnum) – a proper huntsman's sustenance. We were warned that truffling in the Quercynois sense (as opposed to Curnonsky's) is tough, cold, wet work.

Also taking their far-from-*petit-déjeuner* were Lionel Poilâne of the rue du Cherche-Midi on the Left Bank, whom I have long venerated as just about the best baker in the world, and Antoine Zentai, the truffle king of England, who in season commutes between Cahors and London carrying little *coffrets* full of the world's rarest fungi. They both decided to tag along and swathed themselves, like the rest of us, in furs, wellington boots and such odd headgear that rumour went round we were re-enacting the retreat from Moscow.

We were now joined by two hefty sows called Claudine and Diane (truffle hunters prefer female pigs – I was later to learn why), and an even more immense alsatian dog named Hans. There were also three old ladies clutching sticks and wicker baskets. Two of them carried lengths of rope. In addition, there was a stout, shrewd looking, soberly dressed gentleman who, I thought, looked rather out of place. Someone, I felt, should have told him how to dress for the country; at this point, Michel introduced him as Jacques Pébeyre, local landowner and one of the world's great truffle merchants.

Soon we reached a patch of what Monsieur Pébeyre described as promising truffle country. It certainly did not look useful for any other purpose, being (so some of the older members of the party told me) reminiscent of no-man's land in 1917: a few young oaks, bereft of most of their foliage; rough brown soil spattered with weedy grass and splayed with grubby, shapeless stones. The ugly wind was yet another reason why none of us showed much eagerness to leave the conveyance. Excepting Claudine, Diane and Hans, who couldn't wait.

Out they bounced, pursued by their handlers, who deftly sprung nooses round the girls' necks, and we were off.

Now we all know that certain fauna are peculiarly sensitive to the smell of the *Tuber melanosporum*, to give the truffle its suitably unlovely name. I have found this quite easy to believe of dogs, most of whose noses are obviously efficient sensors; but I have always been puzzled about the pigs. After all, a porky proboscis is rather a blunt instrument. Yet here were old Claudine and Diane sniffing obsessively. It reminded me of the Beaunois peasants one sees tasting their annual slug of Chambertin at the municipal tasting.

It seemed a good moment to question one of the handlers, and she drew my attention to the – ahem – gender of Claudine and Diane: the simple explanation is that truffles are redolent of certain important parts of boars. The not-so-good news is that sows don't content themselves just locating the fungi, they want to eat them. The trick therefore was to let them plunge their blunt snouts wildly into that disagreeable soil – they may have to delve three feet – and then at the *moment critique* to haul them back with one hand while digging frantically with the other.

It is different with dogs. What they enjoy is the hunt. Once they have found the tuber, all they want to do is dash off and discover another. More work for the beldam, of course, because she had to dig like fury in order to keep up with the energetic Hans.

Up and down the line of scrubby trees they went, sniffing and digging while the collection of misshapen golf balls steadily increased. For how long, I wondered, have humans realised that these unattractive lumps are capable of contributing fragrant delicacy to any fish or meat? I did not have to wonder for long, for Monsieur Pébeyre is a walking truffolegium. The truffle, I learnt, was certainly appreciated as a delicacy in Mesopotamia (where they still gather them, of the same species as those which grow in England) 2,000 years before Christ. Coelius Apicius used them in some of his recipes; Pliny admired the *terfez* or African truffle, a bulky brute which in early springtime sells in the markets of Marrakesh at about £3 a kilo; despite its subterranean origin, however, botanists maintain it is a mushroom and not a truffle at all – otherwise there would be no Moroccan balance of payments problem.

The English *Tuber aestivum,* on the other hand, is nowadays less prolific. In Victorian times, people in many parts of Britain earned a living from them, and even sent truffles to France. Rudyard Kipling's *Thy Servant a Dog* contains a story about a truffle-hunting mongrel; Gilbert White found some at Selborne; and I remember, a few weeks after the Munich crisis of 1938, that sad subject was driven from the correspondence columns of *The Times* by a spate of letters debating the virtues of the English truffle.

Monsieur Pébeyre said nothing about there being any Germanic truffles, and Peter Kromberg (of the London Intercontinental) and Hans Wismer (the Dorchester) – both inveterate truffle-users – looked suitably downcast.

This prompted my next – slightly tactless – question: were not the white truffles of Piedmont better even than the French ones? Emphatically not, I was told, though the grasping Italians price theirs so heavily that many people think they must be. But try one *en croûte,* or slip strips of it under the skin of a pheasant (Monsieur Pébeyre was evidently citing two staples of his everyday diet) and you will quickly learn what an inferior object it is. Useful for grating over spaghetti, perhaps . . . Happily for them, the Italians do produce a few of the French type (which also are found in some parts of Spain) so God hasn't

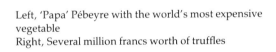

Left, 'Papa' Pébeyre with the world's most expensive
vegetable
Right, Several million francs worth of truffles

135

wholly turned his back – but if they go on dumping wine in French supermarkets, who knows . . . ?

By this time, mesdames' baskets were full, and although the menagerie showed no signs of tiring, our guide decreed that we should adjourn to the town's *marché aux truffes,* where the booty is sold twice weekly, as it has been for 2,000 years – indeed the very weighing scales are clearly of Roman design. Things do not move too fast in Quercy.

My first thought was that we had arrived on a bad day. There were rows of stalls, some displaying massive geese, split open to reveal huge livers; others offered the curious *galettes du sang,* pancake-like black puddings, or the succulent prunes of Agen – but there wasn't a truffle in sight.

A few furtive men with what looked like fishing baskets eyed us suspiciously. This was probably to ensure that we were not inspectors – there is a running battle as to whether truffles are a cultivated product (and the concern of *le taxman*) or *sauvage.* Probably the glamorous Mesdames Mouilleron, Kromberg and Bourdin saved the day, because one of the fishermen slowly opened his basket, revealing several million francs worth of the world's most expensive vegetable. Old francs, *bien sûr*; I said things move slowly here.

The customers appeared equally secretive, rather like the raincoated tourists one used to see discovering souvenir postcards on the Boulevard de Clichy in the fifties. But every now and again some communication was established and a few nuggets were removed and scrutinised, ostensibly for mites – not necessarily a fault, because the maggots are connoisseurs who go for the best. I say 'ostensibly' because everyone is too polite to admit the real purpose of the search, which is for bits of lead – with truffles at £85 a pound, they are a common, but rather unwelcome, additive. In unsmiling discussion, a price per 100 grams was agreed. Grim buyer paid unblinking seller and shuffled off, carrying his purchase as gingerly as an unexploded bomb.

Jacques explained that he did not participate in this poker-faced parody of the United Nations: many peasants simply take their finds direct to the Pébeyre establishment in the centre of town, where each day a notice tells them what he is willing to pay. That department, he said, was presided over by *papa,* so off we went to meet Pébeyre senior, all patriarchal beard and 92 years of him.

Now that we were familiar with the cloying scent of the merchandise, there was little difficulty in finding the depot – indeed, one can only assume that the dogs of Cahors are kept firmly locked up when off duty, or it would not have been possible to get near the place. Here were huge wooden troughs of black and grey 'fairy apples' as George Sand once called them, sorted by quality – this depending on a firm, unbroken surface, not size. I picked up the day's prize 'catch' – it had the texture and bulk of an orange.

It was dusk, and Michel had arranged for us to attend one of the occasional dinners at which chef Patrick Lannes (patron of the Taverne bar where we started the day) prepares truffles in various ways so that the specialists can appraise the season's quality. After a few magnums of Mr Forbes's special and some canapés containing little slivers of some black stuff, we opened with *mille feuille* stuffed with *foie gras truffé,* then moved on to truffles served whole (which Colette said is the only way to eat them) *en croûte,* so help me. I confess to slight relief on being told that we would next refresh our palates with a salad; but it consisted of a mound of sliced truffles with vinaigrette on a bed of greenery. Then there was roast lamb perfumed with you-know-what, *pomme sarladaises* (baked potatoes with truffles) and celery *au jus de truffes.* With the coffee there were chocolates – what *kind* of chocolates, I leave you to guess. A neighbour at table was Georges Vigoroux, an urbane young millionaire who has earned glory by reviving the viticultural fortunes of an old Cahors property, Château Haute-Serre. He had provided two of his vintages and some of the Château's own *marc* – and, to cap it all, invited us to luncheon the following day as he said we ought to taste truffle soup, truffled roast pork (can ingratitude go further?), and truffled sausages. To my shame, I went.

So now I know some of the answers. There are plenty more questions, but then gastronomy is full of mystery: why a particular piece of land in Bordeaux produces great wine while its next-door neighbour, with identical vines, doesn't; why puff pastry puffs, and eggs beat more successfully in a copper bowl than a china one; why the Dutch, who have marvellous milk, make three cheeses which all taste the same, yet their Gallic neighbours can produce over 200 different kinds. But the riddle of the truffle is *hors classe.* Chemically, it consists of a great deal of water held together by granular fungus. It is ugly, warty, and (with respect to boars) smells sickly and unappetising. It grows unpredictably, and continues to defy efforts at commercial cultivation. Yet place a borrowed one overnight in an egg-box: the following morning you can return it to the lender and then make yourself the greatest omelette of your life.

Henry IV attributed to truffles his prowess in the boudoir, and Balzac once said 'if one truffle falls on my plate, it will be enough. It is the egg which hatches ten characters in my *Comédie Humaine'.* What accolade compares with that?

Gunter Brözel

Gunter Brözel – wine man extraordinary *Patrick Grubb*, MW

I was dipping into a book of verse recently, having escaped for a few moments from the clamour of an energetic three-year-old son. Mentally refreshed I returned once more to the fray. I happened upon a few lines which in some slight way set the scene for the man I am trying to portray. In Tennyson's *Maud* there is a verse which says something of Gunter Brözel – a giant among wine makers:

> 'One still strong man in a blatant land
> Whatever they call him, what care I
> Aristocrat, democrat, autocrat – one
> Who can rule and dare not lie.'

Perhaps these lines are too cold and convey a sense of an austere person, one without feeling, but Gunter is above all a kindly man with humour, plainly honest and very human. I met him in 1975 when I visited for the first time in my life the wine lands of the Cape. I had been invited through our office in Johannesburg to conduct an auction of rare Cape wines at Nederburg near Paarl. This was the inaugural sale and I have returned each year in March ever since.

My first glimpse of Nederburg was two days before the auction, when I lunched in one of the cool reception rooms in the old homestead, with a late summer sun blazing down outside. As I arrived with the marketing manager, he said, with a tight grin, that he hoped Gunter would be in a good mood. It was not until much later that I began to appreciate why he might not be. All the spacious lawns hard by the winery were covered with tentage, awnings were rising around the back of the homestead, right up to the winery doors. At the back door it was very much business as usual, as the lorries and hopper trucks lumbered up piled high with grapes from the acres of vines surrounding Nederburg. There were *chenin blanc, colombard, riesling,* and later came *pinotage, shiraz* and *cabernet sauvignon.* All these and several experimental vines produce the grapes that go into Nederburg's pretty extensive range.

All this activity, and at the centre of it, in his relatively small office in one wing of the winery, I was welcomed by the man himself. The first impression is of great physical strength and energy. He is not over tall, with barrel chest, strong hands, a weatherbeaten face and eyes that sparkle with a warming directness. A grin struggles at the corners of his mouth ready to escape at any moment, as he describes his wines. That particular day the greeting was brief. He was busy discussing more pressing items with his assistants, checking must weights, quality of grapes, fermentation temperatures and barely concealing his understandable irritation with the intrusion of the auction.

I did not see him again until the auction was over. A press conference was taking place on the stoep of the homestead. I was feeling rather punch drunk and detached after a marathon gallop through 12,000 cases of Cape wines. The sale had been a great success and in a local context most prices were very high. However, one surprised and disappointed me: the Edelkeur, one of Gunter's especial babies which he had raised first in 1969 as a totally new wine style in the Cape and then nurtured for the commercial market. This was its début and the relative price was about £2.00 a bottle. I should explain that Edelkeur is the Nederburg answer to the Trockenbeerenauslese in Germany, the Late Harvest wines from Chateau St.-Jean and others in California, *Grains Nobles* from Alsace. In all cases the grapes have been affected by botrytis. And of course the superlative Barsacs and Sauternes. The residual sugar in Edelkeur is exceptional, as high as 213 grammes per litre in 1976 with nine per cent alcohol by volume! In 1978 it reached 11 per cent alcohol by volume with a sugar level of 193 grammes. Today the price for this wine at the Nederburg auction is that of Yquem.

Anyway going back to that evening after the first auction. I could not understand the result and with some embarrassment I faced him. His artistic soul bared itself for a moment as he described all the care that had gone into the production of this outstanding wine and finally with tears in his eyes he said that he hoped that the public would become more appreciative. Now, some years later, honour has been saved.

To begin to know and understand the man, it is necessary to go back to his early years in Germany. He was born in Württenburg 46 years ago into a family of fourth generation coopers and vintners. Of necessity in war-ravaged Germany his academic career was rather difficult. There followed a period of apprenticeship as both a cooper and a wine maker under the guidance of his father. He was involved in every aspect of wine making including, as he says with a wink, 'stealing it'! In 1952 he entered the Wine Institute at Weisberg, graduating a year later with distinctions in wine chemistry, agriculture and cellar administration. One of his lecturers has ascribed his success to practical skills, combined with perseverance and purposefulness, characteristics which have continued to distinguish his career. The same lecturer did not mention an occasion when the young student displayed his impish sense of humour. A visiting VIP, no wine expert, was offered a venerable wine of great age and asked 'Who drinks this horribly expensive stuff?' Gunter replied quick as a flash 'Just those who can afford it – and us'.

From the Institute he moved to the Rheingau, where he became the cellar master's assistant, specialising in laboratory work and wine making, for a merchant in Eltville. His avowed aim was to master all aspects of his craft. The next stage took him another rung up the ladder, as a cellar master at a co-operative winery in Baden.

The next and momentous step up was in 1956 when he arrived in the Cape just before the vintage. He had been selected after a long search throughout Germany by Johann Graue, the then owner of and wine maker at Nederburg. Graue's contribution to the Cape wine industry is another story, but he had bought the estate in 1937 and by the early 50s the estate was in a medal-winning class. He introduced cold fermentation techniques for white table wines and ruthlessly culled the vine varieties on the farm until only the most perfect clones remained. He had trained his son, Arnold, to follow him, but tragically this was not to be. In 1953 piloting his own aircraft, the plane crashed and he was killed.

Johann Graue found more than an assistant in the cellar in Gunter; he found someone who shared his goals and would complete the tasks he had set himself. Their philosophy was always, and remains today, absolute quality in wine and in the grapes from which it is produced. Soon after his arrival, Gunter found himself in sole charge of the winery, and has remained so ever since. Two years ago, on the occasion of the opening of the permanent auction centre, a bust of Johann Graue was unveiled by Gunter. He spoke most movingly of the man

Nederburg

who had brought him from Germany and set him at the pinnacle of his profession.

Gunter is not to be envied, but greatly admired. He is responsible for an important profit centre with a market value of the equivalent of nearly £4m and an annual crush of 9.4 million litres of red, white, rosé and sparkling wines. He controls every operation and expenditure. His early upbringing and training in Germany have stood him in good stead. His experimental plantings have had some exciting results, which are now accepted by other growers. He believes in the skilful blending of wines from differing micro-climates on the farms to arrive at a harmonious and attractive whole; I am convinced that he is right. Too often the South African estate wines lack something because single varieties are bottled separately and are too assertive. Gunter is not afraid to admit mistakes and will pursue perfection without sparing himself or his assistants.

I wish I knew more about the man, but his deeds speak louder than words. He is greatly respected among his peers and his awards at international wine fairs make an impressive line up. Despite a very obvious success he is very modest. His contribution to the improvement in viticulture and vinification in the Cape is immeasurable. Nor is he a slouch as a salesman: describing his wine to visitors, both ignorant and knowledgeable, he has the same marvellous simplicity and utter conviction. He waxes lyrical and sometimes becomes quite emotional, but he is always sincere.

I salute you Gunter and wish you and your wife many more years of happiness in your adopted land. I know that you will continue to make others happy throughout the world with your wines.

The scene depicted in this well-known engraving by William Hogarth (March 1732) is St James's Coffee House, Temple Bar. What makes the print interesting is that a number of the sitters are known. The man ladling punch is parson Cornelius Johnson, cousin of Dr Johnson, and the character putting the wig on his head is John Harrison, a tobacconist who had a shop in Bell Yard. On his right is Kettleby, a barrister. The man in the white nightcap is thought to be a chandler who worked for Hogarth. In the foreground is James Figg, the prize fighter reputed to have seldom been beaten but frequently knocked out by Bacchus!

Print collecting and some satirical cartoons of the 18th/19th centuries
Jeremy Roberts

There was a period in my post-school years when I couldn't decide whether to enter the wine trade or the world of fine art. I had an unusual grounding and genuine interest in the latter from an early age. Having spent a number of delightful summer holidays in Paris with a charming family by the age of thirteen I was well acquainted with the Impressionists, Rodin, oriental art and, of course, the massive and overpowering reservoir of art at the Louvre. This was the beginning of an appreciation which has stayed with me ever since.

So it was that at the age of twenty I went for interviews with various well-known publishers, art book and print specialists, but it wasn't to be; I had no formal art training. I then plunged headlong and enthusiastically into a career in the wine trade, but it soon became clear that I would have to take all the basic exams. The obvious tools for the job were books on wine but, hard as I looked, I became aware that there were not that many books available on the subject. Wet afternoons were spent delving into bookshops in London's famous haunts, but all I could find were rather tired copies of Saintsbury, Maurice Healy, H. Warner Allen and, or course, the ubiquitous André Simon.

I wasn't yet collecting consciously, just expanding an interest and, possibly, my career. My first real 'find' came from the New, not the Old, World. In 1963 in New York I discovered one or two sources for old books, many much earlier than any I had seen in Europe. The most important find was a small box of books dating from the 16th and 17th centuries, most in vellum or fine French bindings. True or not, the bookseller told me that the books had been shipped from a library in Amsterdam in 1910 but had never reached their destination. Back in England I contacted André Simon because I had used his excellent reference books, *Bibliotheca Bacchica* and *Bibliotheca Vinaria*, to research my finds. He was a wonderful old man and invited me to his flat to talk. His enthusiasm was enormous and very infectious. In his book, *In the Twilight*, he records how he was offered rare books when there were no funds to pay for them, so something had to be forfeited. He argued that it was always better to spend money on books than on fine wine because books give pleasure for a lifetime whereas the pleasure from the fine bottle is finite.

I was offered a position on *Wine* magazine and, during that period, discovered that it was still possible to find wonderful engravings and even original drawings by famous artists from 1760–1900. I resumed my forays into the print and bookselling world and decided to build up a print reference archive.

Most of my collection has come from bookshops and country auction rooms, where I naturally chased folios containing wine prints. Now and then I have been amazed to discover that the lot contained other drawings and prints of far greater merit than those I had been seeking.

The prints which have given me greatest pleasure have been the satirical cartoons of the period 1770–1820. It was the engravings of William Hogarth, the father of the English cartoon, that I collected first, being attracted by the meticulous detail and the activity of the scenes he portrayed, which give such insight into the 18th-century world. Although Hogarth was a great cartoonist and social critic of his age, he was not a caricaturist in that he didn't distort bodies in quite the same way as Rowlandson and Gillray. Hogarth engravings frequently turn up in antique shops and print sellers, but it is not until one looks at the full-size contemporary folio engravings on hand-made paper that one appreciates his fine draughtsmanship and composition.

Thomas Rowlandson was very different. Not only was he an extremely accomplished artist, but he seems to have been quite a character; a contemporary story has it that he dared to produce a peashooter in the life class at the Royal Academy – with devastating effect. In his late teens he spent some time in France, which may account for the lucidity of his draughtsmanship and the technical ease and elegance which put him in a category of his own.

Gillray was different again. He came from a humble background, his father being a sexton at the Chelsea Moravian community. Like Rowlandson, he too went to the Royal Academy but decided early on to concentrate on lampooning the monarchy, aristocracy and politicians and the fashions and habits of the time. Such was the disturbing effect of his cartoons, which were sold from Mrs Humphrey's caricature shop not a stone's throw from the seat of power, that he was summoned before Bow Street magistrates in January 1796 on the grounds of selling an objectionable print. However, the matter was never tried. It is a coincidence, however, that in the following year George Canning, under-secretary at the Foreign Office, arranged an annual pension of £200 for Gillray on condition that he refrain from lampooning the monarch and politicians so severely. Thackeray is reported to have remarked in 1840 that 'Gillray would have been far more successful and powerful but for that unhappy bribe which turned the whole of his art into an unnatural channel'.

There were other cartoonists working at this time, but Hogarth, Rowlandson and Gillray brought it to its highest art form, paving the way for the next generation. Some of the artists are less well known for there were so many of them as a result of the increase in the number of illustrated journals produced in the earlier part of the Victorian era, for example, *Punch*, the *Illustrated London News*, the *Penny Magazine* and the *Graphic*, to name but a few. George Cruickshank, John Leech, Seymour, Hablot Browne, John Doyle and Gustave Doré were all great illustrators and all, at some point in their careers, illustrated wine. The one name that is perhaps best known to collectors of wine books is that of Henry Vizetelly (1820–94), who was not only a wood engraver and editor, but helped to found the *Illustrated London News*. He is particularly remembered for his five books on wine, all of which were superbly illustrated and give us a good idea of how the wine trade looked in the mid-Victorian era.

Prints and books on wine, pre-1900, are becoming very scarce. I wonder how many people in the wine trade appreciate the artistic worth of some of the pictures and books in their offices?

This cartoon (10 March 1805) is wonderfully evocative of Gillray's draughtsmanship. Pitt is shown as a waiter in the House of Commons pulling the cork from a bottle containing the face of a disconsolate Sheridan. In the background on the opposition benches is a forest of mallet-shaped decanters (bottles) filled with the faces of statesmen of the time.

Pitt and Sheridan were arch enemies in Parliament and the scene was inspired by Sheridan's speech on 6 March 1805 opposing Pitt's additional taxes bill.

Uncorking - Old - Sherry -

Nothing has changed! Raising the duty on wine is by no means a habit of modern governments. This Gillray print of 20 April 1796 shows John Bull's reaction to the duty increase of that year. The figure emerging from the cask is Pitt, decorated with vine leaves, and behind him is Dundas, dressed in tartan as Silenus. The duty increase was £20 per tun or 6d. per bottle, quite a considerable sum in those days. John Bull, stands dejectedly to the right with an empty purse and three empty bottles in one hand.

The WINE Duty, — or, — The Triumph of Bacchus & Silenus; — with John Bull's remonstrance

ANACREONTICK'S in full Song.

This Gillray print of December 1801 shows eight elderly topers singing 'The Anacreontick Anthem'. The constitutional song of the Anacreontick Society used to be sung after supper at the fortnightly concerts held by the Society. The Anacreontick's Society was founded in 1766, the same year as Christie's, and named after the 6th century B.C. lyric poet, Anacreon. The club lasted for forty years, and the membership was made up from all walks of life, numbering amongst its members the Prince of Wales, the Duke of Orléans, noblemen, military officers, learned and professional people. The melody of 'The Anacreontic Anthem' was adapted some 13 years after the appearance of this print to Francis Scott Key's 'Star Spangled Banner'.

Thomas Rowlandson's print was one of a number drawn by him to illustrate 'The Tours of Doctor Syntax in Search of the Picturesque', a book of rather uninspired verse by William Combe, published 1812–20. It is likely that the drawings for this book were taken from sketches made during the artist's ramblings in England and on the continent. In the 1770s he travelled widely and was accorded privilege and consideration and was thus able to observe and draw the life of the period. From these travels he produced a number of sketchbooks, which were later published as 'An Artist in Search of the Picturesque', and it seems likely that 'Doctor Syntax Made Free of the Cellar' could well be himself visiting one of the country taverns on this journey. On close observation one can read the names on the casks in the cellars and from these descriptions it is possible that this was a country hostelry which had reserves of wine or beer for, or named after, the local aristocracy.

Sorting out the seventies

The decade of the seventies
Harry Waugh

When things go well, many of us are inclined to take them for granted; our health is a perfect example. Only when something begins to go wrong do we sit up and take notice. So it is with wine: for instance, has it been realised that the decade under review has possibly been one of the best of the century?

Modern methods of vinification must of course, be taken into account, because vintages such as that of 1973/4 might not have been nearly so palatable had they been handled in the manner of even 30 years ago. Nevertheless, according to the law of averages it is unlikely that the 80s will offer us anything better, although it must be admitted that with the good year of 1981 and especially that of 1982, they have got off to a good start.

What is unusual is that there were really only two weak spots in this decade: 1972 and 1977, but even the '77s, although light, are not disastrous, an example in fact of the resuscitative effect of modern vinification. We have only to think of the '60s, with those deplorable vintages of 1963, 1965 and 1968, to make us count our blessings.

**The 1970 vintage
9/10**

The decade started off in fine fettle with one of those golden years that occur all too seldom: a very large crop of excellent quality. It is rare for such quality to accompany so large a harvest and it was not until some time later that sceptics could accept that it had actually happened.

After a late spring, the conditions throughout the summer and autumn were pretty well ideal; in consequence, just before the vintage began the vines were festooned with bounteous bunches of the most magnificent looking grapes. Nineteen-seventy was also a particularly successful year for the *merlot* vines, hence the success in the districts of St.-Emilion and Pomerol. It was in fact a fine vintage for all districts.

The wines had a lovely dark colour, an attractive bouquet and a fine full-bodied flavour. A drawback, if a temporary one, has been the tannin which has persisted for considerably longer than expected. In common with many others, no doubt, the writer has made the mistake of drinking his lesser 1970s too soon and only now are they beginning to come into their own. For instance, at an epic tasting of 30 examples of this vintage at the Ritz Hotel, London, early in 1980, among six *crus bourgeois* only La-Tour-de-By could really be described as approaching readiness, and even that will improve. The prevailing comment on most of the *crus classés* of the Médoc was 'needs another two or three years'. At a session of some of the great growths held last May (1982) in Rochester, NY, they were still very immature. Tasting them blind, the writer, giving each its correct name, placed them in the following order: Latour (in spite of all its tannin); Cheval-Blanc; Haut-Brion; Mouton-Rothschild; Lafite; Margaux.

The French made a start on their '70's years ago – the British may not have many virtues, but at least we know when to drink our claret!

Even good Fronsadais wines such as Canon de Brem and La Dauphine are still somewhat resistant, but possibly the most enjoyable '70s to drink at the moment are the lesser growths of St.-Emilion and Pomerol. If you can keep your finer growths for a few more years, your patience will be well rewarded – the pleasure is all to come!

The 1971 vintage 8/10

Both for size and quality the crop of 1971 was overshadowed by its copious predecessor; few vintages offer such a cornucopia of plenty as did 1970. In 1971 unsatisfactory weather during the spring as well as the poor flowering of the vines finished all hope of a large crop. Happily the weather was fine at the time of the harvest, but unlike 1970 there was a shortage of *merlot* grapes and among the Médocs there was also some irregularity. Under such circumstances, a skilful merchant can be more useful to one than a knowledge of *châteaux* names. On the whole, the districts of Pomerol and St.-Emilion, especially the former, were more successful than that of the Médoc. For instance, some Pomerols were considered finer than their 1970 counterparts and Pétrus is perhaps a case in point. While their lifespan may not be so long, the '71s have had the advantage of developing faster than the more robust and tannic '70s. The lesser growths should be drunk now, but the greater ones are probably reaching their best and can be enjoyed during the coming few years. The answer is possibly to drink the more successful '73s and '74s first in order to give the better '71s time to show their mettle, then use the latter to fill the gap until the altogether finer '70s are ready.

This vintage improved greatly as it developed and by 1973 some proprietors were even claiming that their 1971 was as good as their 1970; indeed, at a blind tasting held shortly after of the eight top *châteaux*, the four first places were taken by the '71s. As time passes though, the intrinsic quality of the more backward '70s is asserting itself.

At an anonymous tasting organised by the French publication *l'Hotellerie* in November 1982, the result was as follows: Latour, Pétrus, Mouton-Rothschild, Ausone, Cheval-Blanc, Margaux, Haut-Brion, Les Forts de Latour, Cos d'Estournel, Pichon-Lalande, Lafite.

The 1972 vintage
3/10

In spite of good weather during the picking of the grapes, due to wretched climatic conditions during most of the summer the grapes had had no chance to ripen, resulting in some of the most unattractive young wine the writer has ever had the misfortune to taste.

For some years the Bordeaux market had been enjoying an extraordinary boom and by 1972 the growers had begun to think they could ask almost any price for their produce regardless of the quality. Little did they imagine they were about to receive such a rude shock! The exaggerated value at which originally they assessed their '72s finally caused the bubble to burst, the market collapsed and was not to recover for several years.

In order to sell them at all, the price had to be reduced drastically. Although, after some eight or so years in bottle, a few '72s may have lost some of their sharper edge. This is a page which perhaps is better left unturned.

The 1973 vintage
6/10

All the portents had been propitious until, after a cold spell, it began to rain in September, and to such an extent that the grapes swelled almost to bursting point. In consequence the production was vast, mainly rather pallid, washed-out wines, low in acid as well as in tannin. Here, indeed, was a test for the wine makers, and those who were not ruthless in discarding their unsatisfactory *cuves* produced a thin, anaemic liquid.

The successful '73s, namely those with a good colour, although perhaps on the light side, with their attractive feminine charm, have proved very useful. Considerably more successful for the Médoc than either St.-Emilion or Pomerol, many '73s have been delightful to drink, but few will make old bones. One of their assets has been early maturity and if their role has been a fairly modest one, the impact has been agreeable.

The 1974 vintage
6/10

The weather throughout the summer did little to encourage enthusiasm and the harvest was gathered during intermittent showers. Quite a large crop was thus gathered under unfavourable circumstances. However, in spite of their original unpopularity, these awkward, somewhat angular wines have been producing some agreeable surprises.

1974 cannot be classified among the great years, yet in due course it may have something more to say for itself. From early days the quick-maturing '73s displayed their charm, whereas the masculine '74s of a deeper colour, more depth of body, but certainly with youthful brashness, were altogether less appealing. All the same, some proprietors have always preferred their 1974 to the 1973, but for the uninitiated it has been a more difficult year to assess. Some '74s are already very nice to drink and appear to have a longer life ahead of them than the more gentle '73s.

This was one of those rather rare occasions when there was a difference between the Graves district and the Médoc, the red Graves being relatively more successful.

The 1975 vintage
9/10

The 1975s are still closed up and undeveloped. In the early days it was hoped that eventually they would emerge in the rarified atmosphere of 1961 or 1945, if not perhaps at quite so impressive an altitude. There were authorities who predicted they would be even finer than the '70s but, excellent as undoubtedly they are, this optimism has lost some ground.

After a very hot summer, the yield was small and the grapes had very thick skins. This was another occasion when the *merlot* grapes were in perfect condition, the result being an all-round success; a beautiful dark colour, a fragrant bouquet, full-bodied wines with heaps of fruit, but slow to mature. It may be many years before the greater '75s are ready to drink, and treasures such as these should not be touched for some time to come.

The 1976 vintage
8/10

From the bursting of the buds at the beginning of April until the middle of August, the weather was exceptionally fine, warmer and drier than usual. Luckily the vines were saved from the ill-effects of possible drought by some

Harry Waugh, the first Englishman to be honoured, receives the award of the Golden Vine from Norman Gates, Grand Commander of the Knights of the Vine. American winegrower Julio Gallo also received the award

rain in August, with more in September. The vintage began some ten days earlier than usual, on September 15th, and in spite of occasional nocturnal rain, the weather was reasonably good. The production was large and equal more or less to that of 1973 with the quality satisfactory in all districts.

While they have a beautiful colour, the '76s are not quite so dark as the '75s nor so deep or full-bodied, yet they form a delightful contrast. The bouquet is attractive and the wines have a rich, fruity flavour, combined with charm and finesse. They may not be destined for very long life, but what we want is wine to drink now and some of the lesser '76s were already enjoyable by 1980 and at comprehensive tastings held in London in November 1982 and January 1983 they were showing extremely well. This is a vintage which has turned out to be even more useful than expected.

There are some irregularities of course, especially among the lesser St.-Emilions, but on account of its charm and early maturity this is proving an admirable vintage, particularly for restaurants and for institutions such as clubs and colleges.

Happily the price has not increased inordinately and fairly recently, following an anonymous tasting to compare the merits of 1976 versus 1978, leading authorities in Bordeaux were of the opinion that the 1976 vintage, although not necessarily better from the point of view of quality, was certainly of better value with regard to price.

The 1977 vintage 5/10

When vines burst into leaf earlier than usual, they are inevitably subject to damage from spring frosts. In some years, of course, there are few, if any, but misfortune certainly struck in 1977. Successive frosts wrought havoc among the vines, especially the more forward *merlot* plants. Cool weather persisted and resulted in a late prolonged flowering. This meant that when one hundred or so days later the harvest was due to commence, not all the grapes would be ripe at the same time.

Heavy rain followed during July and August, engendering cryptogamic diseases among the vines. In places, the land became so waterlogged as to prevent the use of tractors for the necessary preventative measures. Then came the finest September for over one hundred years, the ground dried up and the vines recovered somewhat, so that in those vineyards which were well cultivated, if the crop was not large at least the vines were healthy.

The vintage began late, on October 3rd, and was gathered in under good conditions. In spite of the rather desperate beginning, the shortage of *merlot* grapes and the fact that some of the *cabernet sauvignons* were not completely ripe, the quality of the wine can at least be described as reasonable.

Nineteen-seventy-seven has been summed up as *une année jalouse*: in other words one of irregular quality, dependent upon the date of picking and the efficiency of individual vinification. Although the wines have a nice colour, they lack body; and while there is some elegance, there is not a great deal more to be said.

1978, the miraculous vintage
8/10

Certainly this vintage deserves such an epithet, because until as late as August 12th the weather had been so appalling that hope of making even drinkable wine had almost been abandoned. From that date onwards, however, the sun reigned supreme in a cloudless sky and that, accompanied by uncomfortably warm nights, helped to ripen the backward grapes. While the *merlots* were of a good size, the *cabernet sauvignons* were very small, with thick skins and all too little juice. As vintages go, this could be described as a very good year for the wines from the Médoc, but less successful perhaps in so far as those from Graves, Pomerol and St.-Emilion are concerned.

The '78s have a lovely dark colour, an attractive bouquet with a good depth of flavour. There is some tannin, but it is not nearly so aggressive as, say, that of the '75s. While the classified growths and better *crus bourgeois* of the Médoc have turned out well, the same cannot be said universally of the lesser wines, especially among the *petits châteaux*. In this particular category, the lesser Médocs of 1979 are probably more reliable.

The 1979 vintage
8/10

More rain fell during March, April and May than in any comparable period since 1946. The buds burst about two weeks later than usual and fortunately, for the second year in succession, there was little or no frost. Continuing poor weather set the vines back further, but even so there were already signs of a large crop. A fine July enabled them to catch up in time for a general flowering around the 20th of that month and that critical period passed off under favourable conditions.

The retarded flowering was responsible, however, for the third late harvest in succession and under such circumstances there is always danger of the weather deteriorating, as indeed was to happen in 1980. July was warm and dry, but August disappointing; more sunshine would have been welcome. The weather remained fine during the vintage, but without the splendid sunshine and general warmth of the previous year. The *merlots* were fully ripe, but the *cabernet sauvignons* would have benefited from more maturity.

That there was going to be an abundant crop was evident, but at the time of the vintage there was little or no excitement regarding the quality. As it turned out, more wine was made in the Médoc than in any vintage since the war. Since no great quality had been expected, the spring tastings produced some pleasant surprises; surprises that have turned to certainty as the '79s continued to expand and develop during the subsequent months.

While this vintage may never be in the class of *une grande année* it is eminently satisfactory in all districts, especially those of Pomerol and St.-Emilion where the wines appear to have greater depth and concentration than in 1978. If anything, the Pomerols appear to be relatively more successful than the Médocs.

It is safe to say that the '79s have a good dark colour and an attractive bouquet, coupled with plenty of fruit and flavour. As they have less tannin than the '78s, they should be ready to drink reasonably early.

Although, generally speaking, the Médocs of 1978 may have more depth and substance than the '79s, there are nevertheless certain *médocain* proprietors who consider their '79 superior to their '78.

Good vintages often run in pairs and as will be seen, this decade has been blessed with no less than three of them, 1970/1, 1975/6. It finished, if not with a great flourish, at least satisfactorily with the two useful vintages of 1978 and 1979.

Since the methods of vinification and changes in oenology continue to improve, future decades will probably fare better still. For instance, the year 1980 will go down in the annals of Bordeaux as the first time that the new *anti-pourriture* treatment was really put to the test. Thanks to the more favourable conditions during preceding years there had been little risk of rot. In 1980, however, but for this beneficial preventative, it could well have been widespread and devastating. When one thinks of the disasters that occurred in 1963, 1965 and 1968, this must surely augur well for the future.

Wine in England during the Reign of Elizabeth I
André L. Simon

Wine in England during the greater part of the reign of Queen Elizabeth I was very much more plentiful than it is today: it was also a great deal less expensive, but there were not nearly so many different varieties as are available now; as to the names of individual vineyards and the dates of various vintages, they were completely ignored.

Although Bordeaux had ceased to enjoy what had been practically a monopoly of tables wines sold in England during the three hundred years of English occupation of Gascony, it still retained a favoured position; by far the greatest quantity of wine imported during the first thirty years of Elizabeth's long reign was red, white and 'Claret' Gascon wine; next, but a long way behind, came the white wines of Charentes vineyards, which were shipped from La Rochelle. Up to 1594, the official or 'Assize' price of all wines from either Bordeaux or La Rochelle was one shilling per gallon, although there is no lack of evidence that one shilling and fourpence was quite commonly the price charged. All other wines were not quite so cheap. Rhenish cost one shilling and eightpence per gallon; Malmsey, Muscadine and Bastard, sweet dessert wines brought to England mostly by the Genoese from Cyprus and other Mediterranean vinelands, cost from two shillings to two and eightpence per gallon; and Sack, the most fashionable wine at the time, varied in price from two and eightpence to three and fourpence per gallon, according to whether it was plain Sack or 'best', and whether it came from Jerez, the chief source of supply, or Teneriffe, or Malaga. By way of comparison, beef cost two shillings per stone, a reasonable enough price, even allowing for a goodly proportion of bones: maybe some of the hide was also thrown in?

All wines imported during the reign of Elizabeth I came in casks, large or small, and of different shape according to their country of origin. There were bottles made of glass at the time, but there were no corks, and bottles were not used to keep or mature wine but merely to serve it. There were large purchases of wine made for the royal cellars and by noble lords with many claims upon their hospitality, but the general rule was to keep on buying small quantities of wine to meet immediate requirements: nobody, not even the Queen, would even dream of 'laying down' wine for future consumption: it was much too great a risk to take. Wine was made then to be drunk within twelve or at most eighteen months, and when it reached that age it was considered to be 'old wine', invariably cheaper than the 'new', most likely because it often had become pricked or flat by then. But 'old wine' had its uses, even before the art of distillation had become popular, in the reign of James I, when it was in great demand to be 'burnt', as they called it, into *Aqua vitae*; during the greater part of Queen Elizabeth's reign most wines which had suffered from being kept in cask too long were used either to make wine vinegar, or else to make Hippocras and a number of cordials in which honey, cinnamon, and other spices covered a multitude of faults.

The greatest contrast of all, when comparing life in England then and now, is, of course, water. There are people who drink water today and they are none the worse for it, but nobody who was not absolutely destitute or desperate dared drink water then. Water was not safe; it was mostly surface water and polluted. Ale for breakfast, before work, and wine in the evening before bed, was what the Queen drank and so did most of her subjects, which accounts for the fact that there was more wine imported for a sparsely populated rural country four hundred years ago than for the teeming millions of present-day industrial England.

It is only fair to add, however, that if the Elizabethans had more and cheaper wine than we have, they had nothing like the same comfort and ease which even the poor, let alone the rich, enjoy today. In their private dwellings, other than those of a very small minority of aristocrats and wealthy merchants, small rooms, low ceilings, slits for windows, no plumbing, little fresh air, lots of foul smells, spluttering tallow dips, incessant canings and scoldings, the whining of

A wine party
by C. de Passe
(c.1550–1643)

sickly children and the howling of lusty ones did not encourage the breadwinner to rush home with all speed when the day's work was done: more often than not he would look in at his usual tavern, where he spent a few pence on wine and an hour or two with his pals.

Vintners, licensed victuallers and taverners, as well as peers of the realm, could have wine on their premises for sale or for their own consumption, but nobody else enjoyed the same privilege. Hence the very large numbers of taverns of every sort and condition: some were mere cellars, with sawdust on the floor, empty casks standing on head that served for tables, and no attempt at anything resembling comfort. But all the more popular taverns were large and commodious houses, with good cellarage below and well-lighted apartments above: the host, and often the hostess as well, welcomed guests as they entered the large public room on the ground floor, directing them to any of the still unoccupied rooms on the next floor, or else to those rooms where their friends were awaiting them. Some of the larger London taverns had twelve of these private rooms, besides the hall on the ground floor.

The quantities of wine sold in taverns to the Elizabethans must have been truly gargantuan: it was all young wine, which was not sipped but swilled in bumpers and at leisure: no time-saving gadgets had as yet been invented to rob men of their leisure. One must also bear in mind that most people were much more dependent then than we are now on each other's company for entertainment: robbers might be hanged and heretics burnt during the day, but at night there were no cinemas, no radio, no television, no crosswords, no canasta. There was, however, more originality of thought, more individuality of opinion, and more earnestness of conviction, all of which helped to make conversation one of the outstanding features of the period. Many who could neither read nor write could talk with charm and wit.

The wine which the Elizabethans drank certainly did them good, first of all because they had great faith in it, which always helps, and it must have cleared their brain and their windpipe, loosened their tongue and their bowels; given them greater assurance in themselves; quickened their receptiveness and sharpened their wit. But all this happened as the sun rises when it is sunrise time, not because the cock crew. They did not drink wine in order that they might talk or sleep better, nor for any set purpose, as a means to an end, but as an end in itself, simply because they liked wine.

Which still is and always was the right approach to wine.

Twenty-one years in the Médoc
Peter A. Sichel

We had lunched at Château Palmer and decided that we would walk the three or four kilometres to the property we had been told was for sale, just the other side of Cantenac. The name meant little to me. Perhaps I had heard of it but in spite of the fact that I had been spending three months a year living as a bachelor at Palmer I had certainly never ventured up the road which leads from Cantenac to Château d'Angludet. The fact that we decided to walk was perhaps our first irresponsible decision in the adventure which was starting for myself and for Diana, who was soon to become my wife. Yes: perhaps in her case it was the second. By the time we had reached Château Prieuré-Lichine it was absolutely pouring with rain. We crouched beneath the arch of the entrance (was I aware of the existence of Alexis in 1961? I'm not sure) for a few minutes before Diana observed, with words worthy of an Alice from the west country, 'Once you're wet you can't get any wetter', so we launched forth again, apparently not getting wetter but certainly with more water pouring off us. That wet walk was our fall through the tunnel which led Alice to her wonderland and ourselves to an adventure which was also far from anything we had previously experienced.

Times had been difficult in the Médoc for some thirty years. Since the late 20s even the best-known wines had been selling at prices which seldom covered production costs. I knew from my father that since his investment in Château

Château d'Angludet

Palmer in 1938 we had had to pour more money into the property each year and most other *crus classés* were forced to sell at least part of the crop months before the harvest in order to cover production expenses. The final straw for many was the severe, long frosts of 1956, which not only decimated the crop but actually killed many vines. Not surprisingly, there were producers who at that time gave up. What was the point in going to the expense of replanting a vineyard if prices being paid for the wine did not even cover production costs. This was the position at d'Angludet. Since 1956 most of the vineyard had been pulled up and most of the land converted to dairy farming. The previous proprietor was also the owner of Château Coutet in Barsac. Because sweet white wines were selling so much better than the wines of the Médoc it was not surprising that when he decided to sell one of his vineyards it was d'Angludet which was put on the market. How things have changed in twenty years.

We were as lucky in space as we had been in time. Isolated, surrounded by woods and fields, a stream flowing 50 metres from the house, a magnificent ridge of gravelly soil which, until the crash of the 1920s, had provided the wines of Château d'Angludet with a fine reputation, the site easily explained why the Chevalier d'Angludet had selected it to build the original *château* when he had discovered it some eight centuries previously. We did not dare to approach too closely on that first visit but skirted the house, picking our way through the waist-high grass, getting only glimpses of the house, which was surrounded by trees. Wet, drab, apparently deserted if not derelict, it was no picture postcard but it was very much the dream of a young couple who enjoyed the country, who wanted to live in the Médoc, to make wine and who, with limited resources, could not hope to purchase a well-established vineyard.

We drew up budgets of course. Certainly not with any pretence of proving that Château d'Angludet was the most viable way of employing available funds – as accountants would have it – but to prove to ourselves and to others that what we had decided was anyway what we wanted, was feasible. Naturally the budgets turned out to be far from reality. Had we known the real figures we no doubt would have gone blindly ahead anyway, trusting that it would 'work out' – though how we could then have persuaded anybody to finance the operation is another question. Lesson number one. If you buy a vineyard in the Médoc, realise that it is a luxury, an investment in a way of life which is your number one priority, not a financial investment.

It is a way of life enriched by that feeling of space which is one of the Médoc's great attributes. Whether it is the broad empty sand dunes to the west, overlooking the endless ocean, the vast expanse of pine trees which stretch southwards to the Pyrénees to form one of the largest forests of Europe, the beautiful fresh-water lakes set like sapphires in the heart of the emerald forests, the wide, muddy but majestic river isolating the peninsula to the east, or the regimented rows of vines under those vast skies which on summer evenings exude a special soft luminosity when the setting sun is reflected by the surrounding water, the scale of nature is always present. To the vastness of space is added that of time. Vines will live at least the space of a human generation – often for the lifetime of him who plants them. Whether businessmen of the 20th century, bankers of the 19th, thinkers of the 18th, princes of the 17th – and even Adam and Eve – careworn people have always found succour in the natural rhythms of a vineyard. Each year the roots dig deeper to produce wines of increasing complexity which in bottle will mature for another generation, immune to all the madness which man seems condemned to create for himself.

Lesson number two: be lucky with the people whom you employ or to whom you go for advice. I had spent a certain amount of time at Château Palmer but really knew little about wine making, less about viticulture. Several years before we arrived at Angludet, Michel and Giselle Chauvet had been 'imported' from Château Guiraud in Sauternes to run the dairy farm and the small remaining vineyard. They had spent most of their life in the Médoc, had no diplomas, but instead a young lifetime of experience, an instinctive knowledge of vines, a loyalty and conscientiousness which are impossible to find if you have to go out to look for them. Then too there was Pierre Chardon at Château Palmer. With roots which have been planted in Cantenac now for five generations, Pierre and his two sons more than anybody have been responsible for the reputation of Château Palmer and there is little he does not know about vine growing in this little corner of the world. For the first few years we remained in partnership with Monsieur Rolland, the previous owner. When the opportunity came to purchase the remaining shares we hesitated. Already we had poured in most of our resources and of course there was still no sign of a return. I shall always remember that large silver-headed upright man putting his hand on my shoulder, looking at me straight in the eye and telling me, 'Do it. With everything you have got, do it. You will never regret it.' He was right, of course, even if the bank manager was less easy to convince.

So on we plunged in our adventure. There are many memories of the early days. Sitting on a pile of rubble with my father drawing plans. Watching the excitement of the specialists as they pulled away rotten skirting boards to discover hoards of very lively insects, including species they had never come across before. Going to see the artist in Bordeaux who had so carefully removed the shredded, faded wall paintings from the *salon* in order to restore them. He rebacked them and went over every centimetre. We had so nearly thrown them out. Now they form the heart of the house, just as they had done, no doubt, when towards the end of the 18th century an artist had been commissioned to copy them from Reidinger's original paintings of the Spanish Riding School in Vienna. We discovered their origin when a friend, Ted Hale, miraculously discovered a calendar reproducing exactly the same pictures.

Memories of our first vintage, of course. We had the right to half the 1961 crop – 6½ hogsheads, 156 cases. It must have been four or five years before we purchased a pump to get the juice and the grapes into the vat. Until then it was carried up a ladder in hods on our backs. The knack was to tip the grapes into the vat without the sudden shift of weight taking you from the top of the ladder with the grapes into the vat. One or two did go in, but we can proudly claim we did not lose a single man! The emotion of the first hailstorm. It takes time to learn to live with nature so I will remember standing in the doorway of the house with Diana, watching the large hailstones being thrown down from the sky with that pitiless force which within seconds strips the vines of leaves and hashes both grapes and wood.

Each year we extended the vineyard, planting two to five hectares per year until we reached the 30 hectares we have planted now, which is near our maximum. We made plenty of mistakes. Not being sufficiently equipped ourselves we had a contractor do the deep ploughing essential before planting. To save time he did not take the trouble to break the impervious layer of alios-compacted sand, which is often to be found in the subsoil. So the roots developed horizontally instead of vertically with the result that those plots are already having to be replanted. The first years, too, we grafted *sur place*, planting the American root stock one year and grafting onto it the following year. This saves time and money when it works but if weather conditions are not favourable there is a greater loss. One year three hectares were a complete disaster, so now we plant with ready grafted plants.

We inherited five or six wooden vats, but they were in pretty bad condition so gradually they were replaced with concrete. There was of course no question in the early days of being able to afford new casks for maturing the wine. Had we had the capital, the wine would have benefited but would we have been able to sell the wine at a higher price? It's not certain. It takes a long time to re-establish the reputation of a vineyard. There are plenty of *petits châteaux* which from time to time put out a wine which in quality rivals that of their more famous

The Spanish Riding School calendar found by Ted Hale

neighbours, but what the market pays for is not only quality, perhaps not primarily quality, but reputation, and that has to be earned over a long period.

Through the 1960s we had little wine to sell. Even those vines planted the first year came into production only in 1964. Anxious to make no false starts, we decided that none of the 1963 or 1968 was good enough to be sold under the *château* name, and declassified most of the 1965 too. By 1969 we still only had 14.5 hectares in production, and it was perhaps in 1970 that for the first time it seemed possible that one day the cash would start flowing in the right direction. Then the tiny crops of 1971 and 1972 helped to bring home a hard lesson of realism. When we had been deciding which root stocks to use we were inevitably asked by the experts whether we wanted those varieties which would yield relatively well or those which could provide less grapes but consequently of higher quality. Naturally we opted for the second. There is perhaps no right or wrong in such a choice but nearly all costs in a vineyard are fixed, so that if the crop is half the normal size the cost of production per bottle will be double. When you are desperately trying to arrive at a selling price which covers your production costs two consecutive small crops can hurt. Certainly it caused an explosion in prices but that was shortlived and it was not long before the two large crops of 1973 and 1974 caused the famous crash.

It was then that we, like so many other growers, started selling direct to the French consumer. We even went so far as to open a stand on the main road in the local village of Cantenac. It seemed a good idea but the neighbours didn't like it. We suspected it was because they had not thought of it first but a delegation was sent to ask us to remove it. We resisted for a while but then complied – we like to think because we were not selling anything anyway. Again the Chardons came to the rescue. Claude Chardon for years had put together a mailing list of people who were interested in buying Château Palmer, or just people who had visited the *chai* and left their name and address. He introduced them to d'Angludet, producing some cash flow at a time when it was desperately needed. It seemed at the time that there was a market only if the price was below ten francs per bottle. It was a long time before we dared to creep above that level.

Vintagers have certainly been the mad hatters of our adventure. We started with locals but as production increased we had to look further afield. We tried gypsies but a particularly nasty knife fight discouraged us from pursuing that route. One year we recruited from the unemployment agency. That was worse and ended in somebody jumping from a first-floor window. Although for the last 30 years Spaniards have provided the backbone of the Médoc's picking force, we have tended during the last ten years or so to have young people, who congregate from all corners of the world. Drawn like bees to pollen they arrive from all directions, some by train, a few in overloaded cars, apparently held together only by their occupants, others by bus, many hitch-hiking. The peaceful roads of the Médoc are suddenly infested with strange looking creatures from other worlds, young people with different experiences of life, most of whom, in spite of their often weird appearance, are frightened neither of work nor of life: New Zealanders who have been working on oil rigs in Canada and who are now, by some quirkish sense of geography, on their way home; Scottish girls who have been teaching skiing in Norway and who are going on to Australia; a family from eastern Europe who come each year to pick grapes and then return behind the Curtain; Americans who have been lumberjacking in Scandinavia; a qualified accountant who gave it up to work Teddington lock but who comes back each year to pick grapes in the Médoc; students from catering colleges; others who cannot find their first job and others whose philosophy is to work for a bit, earn enough to wander on and work again when the cash has run out. They say they rarely have trouble finding work when they want it. All these and more form a heterogenous mob who within a few hours are identifying each other as 'Le Légionnaire', 'Jésus', 'Le Végétarien', La Capitaine', 'Nounours'.

They will spend the next two weeks together, either bent double or on their knees between the low rows of vines alongside local people, Spaniards or strangers from the other end of the world, clipping away endlessly at the bunches of deep blue grapes. Sometimes it will be hot, sometimes wet, their backs will ache, their fingers sometimes will be gashed and will always be sticky and stained from the grape juice. Living conditions are primitive but the food is good, wine flows freely so that noisy evenings will peter out only when Bacchus has compounded fatigue to produce total exhaustion. Having at times cursed their own stupidity for venturing towards a vineyard many swear they will return next year, and some do. Certainly by June of each year we are already having to refuse people.

In many ways our time at Angludet has coincided with the mechanisation of viticulture. At Château Palmer in the late 1950s we were still doing most of the work by hand with horses providing the traction power. One of the advantages of starting from scratch was to be able to plant the rows 1.5 metres apart instead of the traditional metre and thus anticipate the advent of the new generation of tractors which straddle the row of vines and now provide power for almost all vineyard activity. Few realise the amount of attention vines require: pruning, tying up, ploughing, spraying, trimming – most of these operations more than

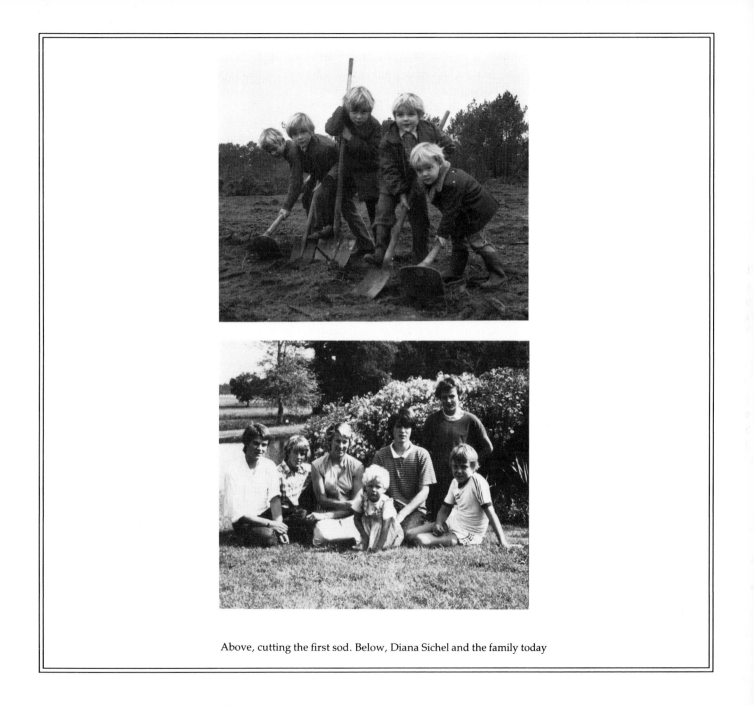

Above, cutting the first sod. Below, Diana Sichel and the family today

once, so that in all each vine has to be attended some 20 times during the year. Much of it can now be done with a tractor, but a good *vigneron* can still prune by hand some 70,000 vines through the winter. The next step will be to abandon the mad hatters for a mechanised harvester. Many have already done so. Often they would prefer to pick their grapes by hand, just as many pickers would be willing to do the job for a wage which makes it economically viable to employ them but *l'Administration*, as the French authorities are referred to, would have it differently. *L'Administration* fills neatly our role of Alice's queen. Though heads are in fact no longer chopped off, the need to interfere and to control persists. Vines cannot be pulled up or planted without an authorisation, bottles cannot be moved from one place to another, papers have to be completed for almost any action. All well meant, of course, all intended to make it a better world, but the mass of regulations and taxes pertaining to employing pickers, to say nothing of the imposed level of wage rates, can only hasten the day when those young people will no longer find work because we will all have been forced to convert to mechanical harvesting.

Twenty-one years in the Médoc have provided an abundance of lessons, some of which are in contradiction to the economic laws that govern the world today. Productivity has constantly to be sacrificed to quality. Every decision which is taken must be directed not towards but generally away from short-term viability, and towards a goal 15 years away or more. Neither caring for the vineyard nor caring for the wine are demanding tasks but both require constant regard to detail. Being passive, neither demands attention. Unlike in an office there is no call to immediate action, but any lack of concern, any prolonged distraction, are harshly punished. This was learned at a time when all my own concentration was being given to a critical situation in our Bordeaux business. Though not apparent at the time it is clear in retrospect that the quality at Angludet suffered as a result. There are no shortcuts possible. The pace is slow but inexorably as the wine matures it will reveal haste, errors or lack of attention which seemed only of marginal importance at the time.

We have learned to live with nature too. Great wine can be made in the Médoc because the soil is unique, but also because the marginal climate leaves all the complexity in the grape. However, for the grapes to achieve full maturity the weather each day is of great importance, particularly as the harvest approaches. Not only hailstorms gave us sleepless nights in the early days; so did those heavy autumn rains which so frequently blow in from the Atlantic to dilute an otherwise promising crop. Our visitors now seem to suffer more from the tension than we do ourselves. We have learned that they are part of life, and to accept them. Less easy to accept is the fickleness of the market place, which one day is clamouring for wine and the next is rejecting it at almost any price. It is never far from our mind that when we started our adventure the Médoc was hardly yet emerging from a depression which had lasted 30 years, that we have had the great good fortune of benefiting from the greatest boom the area has known since the middle of the last century. Where did it come from? How long will it last?

It was perhaps in 1978 that we reached our maturity – appropriately, as it was our 18th vintage. It took that long for the vines to produce wines with the depth of character we had always hoped for, and soon after we were invited to become members of the *Union des Grands Crus* and *l'Académie des Vins de Bordeaux*. We even began too to get letters from consumers asking where they could buy our wine. Achieving some recognition, we were able to invest in some new casks each year, to put the wine in wooden cases instead of cartons and, in short, to achieve in 18 to 21 years what we innocently had thought would take ten. But most satisfying of all is the knowledge that the life of d'Angludet, in spite of its great age, has only begun. Our roots – like those of our vines, will dig deeper each year. We will learn more. No doubt the next generation will have new ideas, better techniques. We are embarking not only on an age of mechanisation but of such techniques as clone selection, which, if properly used, will open new and exciting possibilities. And then there are the woods and the garden. Perhaps a generation or two down the road that will get sorted out too.

Some great German estates
Ian Jamieson, MW

Wine estates, like paintings, should be not judged by the size of the area they cover, but by the quality of the wines they produce. German wine is the result of long uncertain summers, from which real warmth is often lacking. In these circumstances, the micro-climate assumes a tremendous importance. This is one of the reasons why few German vine growers are able to enjoy the satisfaction of gazing upon their property from their bedroom windows while the grapes ripen for a great vintage. The search for the possibility of making the best wine in the region has meant that on many estates the vineyard holdings are often widely separated. This tendency has been increased by the laws of inheritance, which ensure that the children of the deceased receive an equal portion of the estate, however it may be calculated.

The von Schönborn family acquired its first vineyard site in Winkel in the middle of the 14th century. Apart from its vines, the von Schönborns own forests and agricultural land, as well as one of the largest art collections in private hands in Europe.

The list of villages in the Rheingau in which the Domänenweingut Schloss Schönborn has its 65 hectares under vine sounds like a roll call of most of the best known wine names of the region: Hattenheim, Erbach, Johannisberg, Hochheim, Winkel, Geisenheim, Rüdesheim and Oestrich, – all of these villages are capable of making wine at the highest level.

Not far from Schloss Schönborn is the estate of Prince Friedrich of Prussia, based on Schloss Reinhartshausen. Sixty-seven hectares of vineyard, mainly around the villages of Erbach and Hattenheim, are planted up to 80 per cent in *Riesling* vines. One of the characteristics, common to all the great estates is the large percentage of *Riesling* that is grown. Nowadays, wherever a German wine is made from the *Weisser Riesling,* (to grant it its proper name and distinguish it from lesser varieties) the word 'Riesling' will appear on the label. These wines, with their fine acidity, benefit from a period of maturation in wood, which many growers claim to give them. It was a 1911 Riesling Trockenbeerenauslese from Schloss Reinhartshausen that was said to have become the most expensive white wine in the world when it acheived a price of DM 11,000 for one bottle at an auction in Mainz in November 1981. At £73 a sip, it would certainly be a rare experience for most people.

Totally devoted to the *Riesling* vine is the small estate bordering on the river Main, which so pleased Queen Victoria that she allowed it to bear her name from then on. The vineyards of the Weingut Hochheimer Königin Victoria Berg, beyond Wiesbaden, produce a wine with more weight than those of the central part of the Rheingau. Damaging spring frosts do not occur here and emphasis is on 'natural' methods and organic manuring. At the opposite end of the Rheingau, at Lorch, on the 13th-century estate of Graf von Kanitz, no artificial fertilisers have been used since 1968. From the vineyards, covered in straw and sown with grass and clover, elegant, fruity wines are made, including some that are presented dry or medium dry.

This recently revived love of wines with a low sugar content could well be at its strongest at Schloss Vollrads, the castle in the fold of the hills above Winkel. Its owner, Graf Matuschka-Greiffenclau, says that half his crop from the 47 hectares of vineyard is sold on the German market, and half exported. Of his sales in Germany 92 per cent are now in dry or medium dry wines, and the Graf seems convinced that well-made German wine with the minimum of residual sugar can provide as happy a marriage with food as any. As if to prove the point, he has converted into a restaurant the Graues Haus, in Winkel, owned by his family for 800 years. A range of 120 Riesling wines from many different growers in the Rheingau is available.

In the last few years, Schloss Vollrads has exchanged views and information on wine matters with another great estate based on Wachenheim in the Rheinpfalz region –that of Dr Bürklin-Wolf. In comparison with the Greiffenclaus at Schloss Vollrads, the Bürklin-Wolfs are relative newcomers, since they have been making wine for only 400 years. On their estate one is aware of the attention to every detail that derives from devotion to quality wine production. The different vine varieties are made, matured, and sold individually, and no advantage is taken of any latitude in blending allowed by the law. In common with other fine Rhineland estates, the minimum legal must weights for the various categories of wine (Kabinett, Spätlese etc) are regarded as reference points only, and are regularly exceeded by Weingut Dr Bürklin-Wolf. The wine maker is Dr Georg Raquet, formerly director of the state domain at Niederhausen-Schlossböckelheim in the Nahe valley.

When thinking of great Rhineland estates, most of us turn first to the Rheingau. In the approximately 2,800 hectares under vine in this region there is probably a greater concentration of old-established wine producers than in any other part of Germany. Not all of them are well known but few would be worth passing by. Possibly because of this, one's attention can easily be diverted from the outstanding wines of the middle Nahe on the opposite side of the Rhine. A leader in this region is the Staatliche Weinbaudomäne Niederhausen-Schlossböckelheim mentioned above. Its owner is the federal state of Rheinland Pfalz. In the UK, state ownership often unfortunately suggests underfunding, inefficiency and low standards. In Germany, it is quite the opposite as far as wine production is concerned. The domain at Niederhausen-Schlossböckelheim, with its 45 hectares of prime vineyard, shows what can be achieved by money, expertise and a dedicated cellar master. Besides making elegant, racy Riesling wines, the domain plays an experimental role in vine growing and wine making matters. It sells its wine directly to private customers, and to the wine trade via brokers. These are the usual outlets for German estate-bottled wines, to which may be added in certain areas, industry, military messes and better quality restaurants, (nobody claims to supply mediocre restaurants!). Many of the smaller growers own a wine bar through which they may promote their own wines, but this is not normal practice on the great estates.

Being big may be beautiful, and sheer size can be impressive when it comes to vineyard holdings in the best sites. To the wine lover the size of an estate is of interest, but more to the point is the quality of its wine. Judged by size, the 12.5 hectares of Nahe vineyard owned by Weingut Hans Crusius near Bad Kreuznach may seem unimportant to anybody more familiar with the massive wineries of California. However, the average size of vineyard holding in Germany is only just over one hectare, and the Crusius reputation has been achieved by running a 'tight ship' well. The Riesling wines from the Bastei

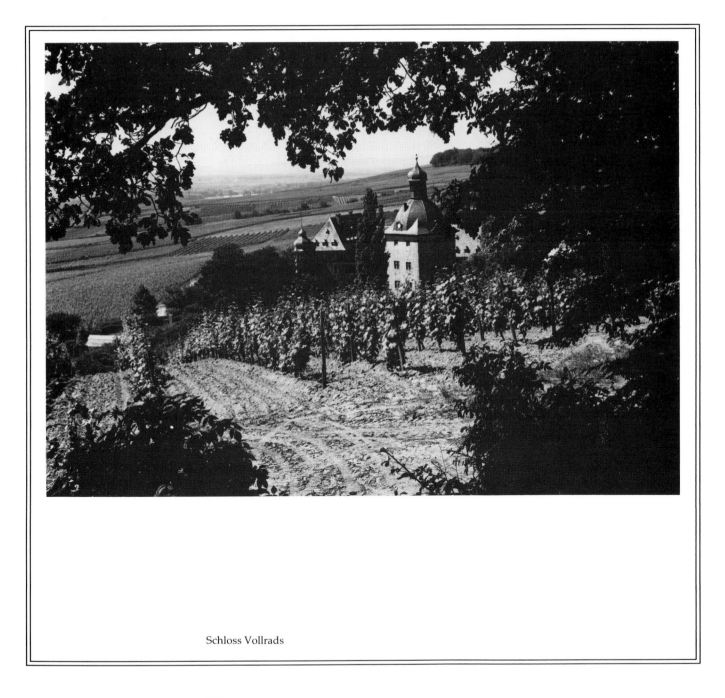

Schloss Vollrads

vineyard, at the foot of the massive Rotenfels – the red rocks that reach hundreds of feet into the sky outside Bad Münster – have a concentration and intensity of flavour that originates in the soil. They are guided to perfection by the attention of Herr Crusius himself.

Some estates rely on a distinguished past to publicise the good quality of their present-day wines. This often results in a somewhat romantic approach that is difficult to resist in an ancient, vaulted, candle-lit cellar. One should remember, nevertheless, that behind the genuine old-world facade, there is almost certainly a battery of stainless steel vats, with all the paraphernalia that a marriage of traditional and modern wine production requires. The wine maker will not be some ancient red-nosed Bacchus, but a highly qualified *Weinbauingenieur*, with much theoretical and practical experience. A number of estates like to emphasise their technical approach to wine production, and hand their customers an 'Expertise'. This is a document, usually signed by the cellar master, giving the full history of the wine from grape to bottle, including a chemical analysis and, if applicable, the marks achieved in the major state wine-tasting competitions.

The great estates are run by knowledgeable men who are totally *sérieux* in their work. This need not automatically exclude a sense of humour or, indeed, downright eccentricity. One owner of a well-known Rheingau estate likes to accompany his tastings with music, changing the record to suit the wine. Thus, wine number one may be accompanied by Schubert's Trout Quintet, and the last, a 1976 Beerenauslese, proves a resounding success, supported by the end of Act 1 of *Aida*. This seems to set a very dangerous precedent, for if the marriage of wine and food can prove problematic, think what imagination will be needed to match accurately a vivacious young Mosel with appropriate food and the right *spritzig* music. Blind tastings are sometimes dreaded, but deaf ones seem to have much to be said for them!

A few German vineyards are entitled by law to sell their wines under their own names without the addition of a village name. One thinks of the state-owned Steinberg site in the Rheingau, and of the Scharzhofberg at Wiltingen on the Saar. Certainly since 1797, one of the best known of the part-owners of this famous vineyard has been the Weingut Egon Müller. The garden of the solid 19th-century estate house leads straight to the foot of the steep vineyard itself, with its rows of well-tended vines climbing up the slope. In great vintages, the Egon Müller wines are amongst the very best, and are built to develop in bottle over many years. A 1964 Scharzhofberger feinste Auslese of Egon Müller impressed at a tasting in Germany in 1977 by its freshness, finesse, and 'noble acidity'. These are the characteristics to look for in fine Saar wine.

Left, Schloss Johannisberg
Above, Hans Crusius in his cellar at Traison

Another part-owner of the Scharzhofberg is the Hohe Domkirche in Trier, now combined with two great estates also of ecclesiastical origin, the Bischöfliches Priesterseminar and the Bischöfliches Konvikt, to form the formidable Bischöfliche Weingüter. At the vintage, the must from the vineyards on the Saar, Ruwer, and the Mosel is brought to the central cellars near the cathedral in Trier, for fermentation and maturation in wood. Dr Hans Ambrosi, the author and director of the state cellars at Eltville in the Rheingau, has described the 400-year-old, fully modernised cellar as a model to others. So be it!

Downstream from Trier at the mouth of the Ruwer is the Weingut Eitelsbacher Karthäuserhof. It may not benefit from the divine protection presumably given to the Bischöfliche Weingüter, but is vineyards do enjoy the offerings of over 50 Trakehner horses, bred by the owners of the estate, Maria and Werner Tyrell, to produce a 'tough, characterful, uncomplicated animal as a friend for riders of the future'. Not surprisingly, the estate can claim that the soil of its vineyards is rich in humus but even if this is insufficient to retain moisture in a dry summer, a water sprinkling system can restore the balance.

As elsewhere in Germany, all the great estates on the Mosel concentrate on the *Riesling* vine, and value a certain amount of maturation in wooden casks. Their vineyards are found on the steepest slopes, at a gradient of at least one in five. Such terrain produces a relatively small yield, and concentrates the flavour. This is especially true in the two most reputed sites of the middle Mosel, the Bernkasteler Doktor and the Wehlener Sonnenuhr. The firm of Deinhard owns part of both, as well as enjoying holdings in other top quality vineyards in the immediate district, and at Kasel on the Ruwer. Deinhard's interest in fine estate-bottled wines does not in fact end there, for in all it owns 100 hectares that cover the Rheingau, and Rheinpfalz as well. The aim on its three estates is to produce refreshing, stylish wines, typical of site and vine variety that benefit from bottle age. At the turn of the century a vineyard worker could hope for a wage of about two gold marks per day. Deinhard's acquisition of a major share of the Bernkasteler Doktor in 1900, at a cost of 100 gold marks per vine, was amazing then and still seems remarkably high when converted into today's terms. Such was the cost of one of the best vineyard sites in the world.

The huge range of wine in many different categories individually offered by German estates may seem to be a commercial disadvantage to the producer. He must sometimes envy the owner of a Bordeaux *château* who may well have one wine, and one wine only, to sell. However, it is surely variety that holds the interest of the wine enthusiast, and the fact that there are so many splendid German estate-bottled wines to be tasted is cause for rejoicing.

Above, ruins of Burg Metternich near Ellenz
Left, the vineyards of Königin Victoria Berg

California classics *Bob Thompson*

Iron Horse vineyard

New vineyards sprout, it seems, from every hill and dale in coastal California. Almost any impressive building under construction in the countryside will, on examination, turn out to be a new cellar. It has been so since 1972.

The prospect is appalling to form players, who could and did coast through the 1960s knowing for certain that six to a dozen labels yielded all the classic wines a collector had to have. Beaulieu Vineyard, Heitz Cellars, Inglenook, Charles Krug, Louis M. Martini and, perhaps, Souverain for Cabernet Sauvignon; for Chardonnay, the knowing bibber went to Hanzell, Heitz, Stony Hill, Charles Krug and, towards the closing hours of the decade, Chalone. On those rare occasions when Pinot Noir rose to the heights, the bottles came from Beaulieu, Chalone, Hanzell, Heitz, and Martini.

Oh, the rare surprise would come from elsewhere, but a collector could earn full marks for thoroughness as well as skill by sticking with that short list year after year. The true believer would round out his cellar with some Johannisberg Rieslings, Zinfandels, and the odd Barbera, but not at the expense of adding any different labels.

Where does the confident collector of 1968 turn in 1983? In circles.

Not only do names come (and, even more, go) with dizzying speed, but the very definition of 'classic' is under assault as newcomers explore new styles in search of a distinct identity. Still, the questions will not go away. Who are the new classicists? Which are the new classics?

As a starting point, it must be remembered that California is still California, still something of a frontier where wine makers matter as much or more than vineyard properties. In most regions in the state, a first-rate man can win out using less than the finest vineyards in the neighbourhood, perhaps far less. Only in the Napa Valley, years ahead of the others at sorting out its vineyard lands, is it no longer enough to be an outstanding wine maker. Grapes for the finest wines must come to skilled hands from favoured places. While several superlative wine makers in the valley regularly outstrip lesser talents unable to capitalise on superior vineyards, they cannot start with a very long handicap.

California is still California for a second reason, that it offers an impressively different environment for the vine from that of France or Germany. To descend for a moment into what Hugh Johnson calls wine newspeak, California's sunny warmth gives riper grapes that make wines typically having higher alcohol (13.0–14.5 per cent in California as contrasted with 11.5 per cent in Bordeaux to sugar-aided 13.0 per cent in Burgundy), higher pH (3.3–3.6 compared to 3.1–3.4), and somewhat different acidic content (not so different in numbers as in character). For bibbers this translates into headier wines of softer contours than European counterparts, even when a California wine master tries to restrain nature. California sunshine at full strength produces blockbusters, some fascinating, a majority boring, all hard to drink all the way through dinner without falling asleep in the salad.

Too many of the new wave of critics have been seduced by these blockbusters, and too many of the new wave of wine makers have believed the critics. The upshot is that too many of the 1970s wines hailed as classic are, instead, merely gigantic. Fortunately, some wine makers never lost the way. Better yet, at least a few of the wayward have begun to notice that overblown wines from the 1970s are ageing less attractively than modest ones from the 1960s. Indeed, a surprising number of Cabernet Sauvignons from the 1970s are now older and more tired than merely better-than-average ones from the 1960s. Some seem wearier than the best from the 1950s.

If ability to age is part of being a classic, and I think it is, then the odds seem to favour wine makers who have grown up with wine and grapes, or at least farming. Not every time, but often enough, they seem to work with a more balanced view than those who arrive as amateurs. If another part of the definition is that a classic wine has to have the power to kindle and rekindle interest from first glass to last sip, the edge still goes to old hands. Not old labels.

Old hands wherever they are. Put another way, the earthy souls who set out to make good, dependable wine often end up with something grand while those who aim at the stars usually hit something else.

The list of prospects ranges widely. To keep the discussion in bounds, I have passed over sparkling wines and botrytised white Rieslings, and limited myself to Chardonnay, Pinot Noir, Cabernet Sauvignon, and Sauvignon Blanc.

Chardonnay

Students of French wines have no trouble accepting Chardonnays called Chablis, Le Montrachet, and Pouilly Fuissé as different, not only because they are, but also because they have different names to announce the changes. Students of California Chardonnays, faced with a similarly broad range of character and style, are handicapped by an absolute lack of signposts, so struggle to decide which of the nameless styles are classics.

The search centres on wines full of flavour, partly from well-ripened grapes, partly from new or almost new barrels. One school of thought looks to wines from very ripe grapes, soft-textured, full-bodied from the resulting alcohol, and redolent of fruit. Such wines come from vineyards towards the warmer end of the spectrum, which give the needed high sugars. The opposing school seeks wines from less ripe grapes, ones with more subdued but hardly neutral fruit flavours and a crisper feel from higher acids. Cooler growing conditions best reward the theory. Both schools look to oak flavours for added complexity, some with a vengeance, some with caution.

Stony Hill and Charles Krug 1968s and a Hanzell from as long ago as 1957 still croon the truth in 1983. For durable vitality, California Chardonnays should be picked while the grape flavours still smack of apples or peaches rather than after the decadent notes of pineapple and other jungle fruits set in. Oak wants a light hand, always. As contrasting evidence, many tropically ripe, oak-laden titans from 1978 have been dramatic, worth experiencing, but they totter towards senility already. Some 1980s that are fine now do not seem disposed to make old bones, either.

Of the old guard, Stony Hill in the Napa Valley, Hanzell in Sonoma, and Chalone in Monterey continue little changed, although Hanzell has struck for a somewhat riper style in recent seasons. Heitz Cellars has not been in the race these past few years for lack of the vineyards Joe Heitz favoured (one was replanted to other purposes, the second temporarily lost to Pierce's disease), but he anticipates being back on course in the next year or so.

Among the newer names, three in particular seem to help define classic: De Loach, Freemark Abbey and Trefethen.

1980
NAPA VALLEY
CHARDONNAY

PRODUCED AND BOTTLED BY
FREEMARK ABBEY WINERY, ST. HELENA, CALIFORNIA, USA
Alcohol 13.5% by volume

Freemark Abbey's Napa Valley Chardonnays call to mind the old Hanzells, and no wonder. Brad Webb set the style for both. That style has a welcome austerity about it, a quality that demands the palate pay attention to arresting textures as well as tastes. The Trefethen Napa Valleys made by David Whitehouse are quite the opposite, silken wines that slip away trailing luscious perfumes as reminders to have another glass. Cecil De Loach is a compact, commonsensical man not given to poetic description, but his De Loach Vineyards Sonoma Chardonnays fit exactly between Freemark nubble and Trefethen sheen, and are, to my mind, suited exactly to the fresh foods that shape cooking in northern California.

Chateau St. Jean comes up in any discussion of California Chardonnay, but there are so many, from vineyards in such scattered parts of Sonoma, that it is hard to pin them down. Time soon should tell which of Richard Arrowood's vineyard-designated wines are the classics, or neo-classics, for they seem particularly Californian.

Dozens of others clamour to be included in any listing of classics. From Napa, the well-established Beringer and Robert Mondavi, and new names Acacia, Monticello and Vichon must be considered. All save Acacia draw heavily from vineyards at the north boundary of the city of Napa, not far from Trefethen. Acacia, under the direction of Mike Richmond, uses grapes from Carneros, two or three miles to the south. Richmond, incidentally, acquired his sense of style from Brad Webb during a stint at Freemark Abbey, and thus makes a case in point of an old hand behind a new label. The Sonoma Valley has contenders for top honours in Hacienda and, at its best, a resurgent Buena Vista. The Russian River region has promising newcomers at Balverne and Sonoma-Cutrer. (I champ in particular to taste the first Sonoma-Cutrers, from 1981. The wine maker is Bill Bonetti, who played a major role in Krug's heyday, and who has one proven vineyard near De Loach, another in the near neighbourhood of Hacienda.) In the cool westerly part of Mendocino County, Edmeades has shown some signs of classical style to go with appreciable substance. The central coast counties of Monterey, San Luis Obispo, and Santa Barbara are enigmas for lack of track records. A skilled wine maker named Ken Brown has made several stunning Chardonnays for Zaca Mesa, in the Santa Ynez Valley of Santa Barbara County. These could be classics if they age true to type. In the adjoining Santa Maria valley, a vineyard called Tepusquet seems to have the right stuff, but still is waiting for the right winery to grab hold. At Jekel, on the Salinas Valley floor far below Chalone, a young wine maker named Dan Lee made several delicious Chardonnays before moving elsewhere, but I cannot anticipate what will come of them with time. In their succulent, almost sweet youth they make me think that this is what would happen if the Germans could get Chardonnay to ripen.

Pinot Noir

As long ago as 1895 the legendary scientific researcher Eugene Waldemar Hilgard wrote off Pinot Noir in California. The doomsayers have not relented since, and still wine makers fight the brave fight, winning it just often enough to find another thread of hope, tatter of courage, stroke of inspiration.

Although prospects are brighter than ever before, much progress is being overshadowed by wild experiments with extra-ripe grapes, superheated fermentation, fermentation with this or that proportion of stems tossed into the pot, and I don't know what all else, but surely some unusual approaches to barrel ageing. Revolutionary ideas be damned. Pinot Noir must be coaxed more than other wines, but the future looks to lie far more with conventional wine making, much of it – antithesis of Burgundy – from vineyards close to tidewater.

Of those with long records, Chalone has stayed on course, perhaps the closest echo California has to Burgundy. Hanzell continues to make splendid Rhônes from the grape. Louis M. Martini still rises to the occasion more often than many realise, primarily with grapes from the Carneros district at the cool, bay end of the Napa Valley. But the majority of hopes for classics are with newer cellars, which seem to control the vines closest to salt water. Acacia, using only grapes grown in Carneros, has made some remarkable though distinctly oaky wines. Three neighbours near the western Sonoma County town of Forestville have signalled that this just might be the right place. Forrest Tancer at Iron Horse, De Loach (again), and Tom Dehlinger have all made wines that have at least some of the hallmarks of classics. An exception to the sea air theory, tiny Calera, on the opposite slope of the Gavilan Mountains from Chalone, has produced its first few hundred cases of Pinot Noir, and haunted palates with the harmonies.

There is but one earnest bit of advice. Have some patience. It takes fine California Pinot Noirs about six or seven years to compose themselves. Those who drink and dismiss them earlier miss their point.

ALCOHOL 19½% BY VOLUME

CALIFORNIA
MUSCATEL
MADE & BOTTLED BY
Louis M. Martini
ST. HELENA · NAPA COUNTY · CALIF.
Distributed by Barrott & Co., San Francisco, Calif.

Cabernet Sauvignon

In another colour, in another key, the story of Cabernet Sauvignon is the same as Chardonnay's. Restraint at the beginning leads to huzzahs down the road.

Somehow the idea got implanted that because first-rate Médocs are undrinkable for their first few years, so California Cabernet Sauvignons should be. Throughout the 70s impassioned newcomers drowned us in inky juices with enough tannin to cure a cow's hide. If such wines change, it is never for the better, or at least not enough. Among them are the only healthy, sound wines in the world I would rather add to the burdens of the next generation than drink myself. Now tannin is going out and the profligate use of *merlot* as a blend grape is all the rage. Delicacy remains too little discovered by too many of the starry-eyed.

When I grope around the darker corners of my cellar to pull out one of the splendid survivors from the 1960s or 1950s, keen anticipation always has a companion recollection of how appealing and harmonious the wine was as a youngster. The 1969 Heitz Martha's Vineyard, the quintessential California Cabernet Sauvignon, presently is as plump and intricate as a statue of Buddha. It always was. The 1955 Louis M. Martini Special Selection has a limpid grace as close to claret as this state ever comes. It always did. When I grope around my wine merchant's for new classics, such recollections haunt me, but comparable wines are scarcer than the swollen number of labels leads me to expect.

For all my plaints, Cabernet Sauvignon still is California's finest red, and there are more classics, neo-classics, and emerging candidates of this variety than any other. Not surprisingly, in view of the span of years it takes an age-worthy red to lay down a record and the brevity of Cabernet's history in the rest of the state, nearly all of them come from Napa and Sonoma wineries.

Surprisingly few of the old guard continue in top form. Heitz does, and has found the splendid Bella Oaks Vineyard to run as a stablemate to Martha's Vineyard. Meanwhile, Inglenook has dropped off the pace, Souverain is no longer the winery Lee Stewart made it, and Beaulieu Vineyard has become a slight enigma. BV's Georges de Latour bottlings start off rich and complex, but recent vintages have not been ageing as long as their forebears did, and do.

Two that remain very fine tend to get shouted down by the gigantists. Charles Krug Cesare Mondavi Selection bottlings remain more than mildly estimable, but all too often go overlooked. So do Louis M. Martini wines, although I suspect this will change soon. Michael Martini is now reaping the rewards of almost 50 years of careful vineyard development by the family. Individual vineyard bottlings, beginning with a 1978 Monte Rosso, promise to live with the 1955s, 1964s, and other indefatigables from two earlier generations of Martinis.

Other wine makers have joined this gentle school. Bernard Portet of Clos du Val frankly makes his Stag's Leap district Cabernets to have early charms, the lightness of his native clarets rather than the solidity so recognisable as Californian Cabernet. Though it was not his original intent, the tantalisingly complex charms are proving durable. Caymus, where Chuck Wagner is the second generation on a family property east of Rutherford, has some of the same lightness, but more straightforward aromas of the grape. Warren Winiarski, at

RUTHERFORD HILL

1976
NAPA VALLEY

GEWÜRZ
TRAMINER

Produced and Bottled by
RUTHERFORD HILL WINERY, RUTHERFORD, CALIFORNIA
Alcohol 12.8% by volume

Stag's Leap Wine Cellars, takes a bare trace of a step farther towards traditional Napa fleshiness, but he does it by restraining tannin more than with riper grapes (except for Cask 23, which always has the scent of fully ripe grapes about it).

Beringer, a renascent old-timer, has produced a sequence of richly scented, full, beautifully balanced Private Reserves from Lemon Ranch, a small vineyard tucked away in gentle hills at the east side of the Napa Valley. Wine makers Myron Nightingale and Ed Sbaragia have other resources of similar promise. Rutherford Hill also has produced some memorable Cabernets in the same fleshy, full-flavoured vein. With them wine maker Phil Baxter reinforces the old Martini lesson, that vineyard blending can be more than a minor virtue in California. Conn Creek belongs in this company. In the Sonoma Valley, Steve MacRostie at Hacienda Wine Cellars has produced a sequence of excellent Cabernets of similar style but distinctly different grape character.

Two other Sonomans have begun making a case for growing Cabernet Sauvignon at the mouth of Dry Creek Valley, just west of Healdsburg. David Stare at Dry Creek has made several supple Cabernets that are attractive early and seem poised to age well. Charles Richard has offered only two vintages at his property, Bellerose, each containing all the red grapes common in Bordeaux. Although some fine points of style remain to be resolved, both wines promise pleasure for years to come.

Paul Draper brought lessons learned in Bordeaux to Ridge, and has applied them with grave intelligence to grapes from several regions but especially the winery's own Monte Bello Vineyard, on slopes high above southern San Francisco Bay. The wines have much of the austerity of, say, a Pauillac, to go with their Californian qualities, so they do well with European tasters. However, and it is dramatic measure of Napa's dominance in local perceptions of what Cabernet should be, three of four medals awarded to Ridge Cabernets at major competitions were for wines from a Napa vineyard, York Creek. It is another measure that, aside from Ridge, no other winery south of San Francisco has managed to carve out a solid reputation for Cabernet or any of its kin. Fred Brander may change that at his cellar in the Santa Ynez Valley, but with a blend dominated by *cabernet franc* and *merlot* rather than *cabernet sauvignon*.

All of this leaves out only one name surely belonging in the list of classicists, and that – back to Napa – is Robert Mondavi. Tim Mondavi, as wine maker, has made a sequence of delicious wines. But, with the endless Mondavi willingness to experiment, one is hard put to pin them down for style. Suffice it to say that he is a one-man demonstration that any definition of classic has a great deal of room within its bounds to accommodate individuality.

Sauvignon Blanc

Sauvignon Blanc has had a difficult time acquiring status as a classic, partly because the French have not managed to make enough legends at their end to provide a real impetus, and partly because the American market place seems to have a hard time accepting two classics at a time in any one colour. The net effect is that a majority of California wine makers opt for quick-ageing, easily approachable styles. Be that as it may, some California Sauvignon Blancs (or Fume Blancs, as they are alternatively known) merit the status of classic by all points of the definition.

The original lessons came from Wente Bros, whose Livermore Valley vineyards seem the perfect environment for rearing long-lived, multi-faceted wines of the type. The 1952 and 1966 both lasted 15 years with distinct flavours of the grape, and would have gone 20, I think but can't know because I got impatient.

The Wentes got tired of waiting for bibbers to discover that patience was the name of the game, and now make early maturers. The contemporary hopes of classicists rest with Brander, Dry Creek, Kenwood, Santa Ynez Valley, Sterling, and Vichon, the latter another new label directed by a wine maker with family ties to the vine going back before Prohibition. Fred Brander (of both Brander and Santa Ynez Valley) and George Vierra of Vichon each use substantial proportions of *semillon* and a light kiss of oak to complicate lean, austere wines. (The Vichon is almost 50:50, and thus known as Chevrier Blanc.) David Stare at Dry Creek and Bob Koslowski at Kenwood elect more straightforward approaches to Sauvignon Blanc. None has been on the track as long as the Wentes. Dry Creek, the oldest, has a 74, nearing the end now, which smells enticingly of a whole Italian delicatessen for reasons I do not understand but admire.

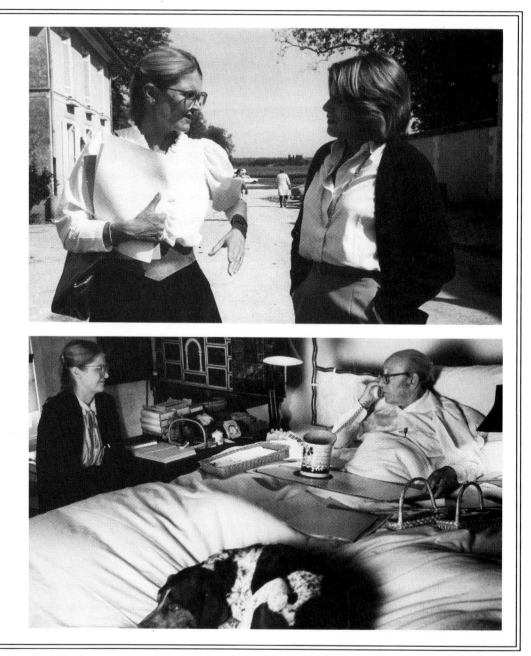

The author with Corinne
Mentzelopoulos at Château
Margaux

With Baron Philippe de
Rothschild and friend

The Wine Programme
Jancis Robinson

In the autumn of 1980 a film producer met a man in a pub and went home with him to try a bargain bottle of Boisset Rouge. The consequence was *The Wine Programme*, Britain's first television series on wine, shown last summer on Channel Four and written and presented by this rather bemused wine writer.

To those of us convinced of wine's eternal fascination, it had long been a mystery why the subject had been largely ignored by a medium apparently obsessed with serialised soap, but prepared to give so much precious airtime to interests such as cookery and antique collecting. (I have since discovered the explanation, by the way. Wine projects never got off the ground because the television high-ups were convinced the subject was too élitist, or so important it couldn't possibly be entrusted to anyone other than themselves.)

Barry Hanson, producer of tough dramas such as *The Naked Civil Servant*, and *The Long Good Friday*, decided to do something about this sad state of affairs when he found himself driven out of his Chiswick local by the house red wine in the company of a neighbour who turned out to be TV producer Tim Aspinall. Fuelled by Tim's special buy, they came up with all sorts of ideas for putting wine on the screen (including a horror movie to be called *The Killer Vintage*) and started looking at books on the subject, a couple of them by me.

According to Barry Hanson – in his cream suits, pale leather pumps and flat cap, a most unlikely figure for the wine world – they thought this Jancis Robinson person was 'probably some old bloke of middle European origins'. I disabused them of this when summoned to Barry's office early in 1981, just as he was being set up by Goldcrest Films and Television, the company behind *Gandhi* and *Chariots of Fire,* to make educational films which took the fancy of both him and television's new Channel Four. There just *had* to be a series on wine.

We fast came up with a title by combining the rather obvious inspiration of my first book, *The Wine Book,* with a suggestion from the now defunct *Book Programme.* The fact that Goldcrest is a subsidiary of the mighty Pearson Group made *The Wine Programme* a relation, albeit distant, of Pearson's little property in the Gironde and gave rise to a phrase that was to be used shamelessly when trying to explain this new project to the bewildered wine trade: 'Goldcrest – you know, Château Latour.'

The next step was to 'shoot a pilot', something I'd hoped I could leave hi-jackers to get on with. But no. There I was one cold January night, knee-deep in a barrel of expensive greengrocer's grapes in a Surrey garage explaining earnestly to a camera lens how to make wine in general, and in particular how one Italian family in Sutton does it each September. *Cinéma* not exactly *verité* admittedly, but we did want to keep everything (other than my poor purple ankles) jolly.

We all felt strongly that we wanted to present a series of programmes which would tell the story of how wine is made and can best be enjoyed in an entertaining and stylish way, but without patronising or riling the (as yet potential) viewers. Not for us the scene on the vine-shaded terrace in which J. R. and Le Comte de Bonnebouteille indulge together in one of the Count's finest vintages, smugly lamenting the fact that no one 'out there' could savour the same pleasure. We were trying to present a *Teach Yourself Wine* in all those wonderful aspects that **can** be transmitted visually.

Paul Fisher was engaged as producer/director and treasured for his all-too-short status as relatively untutored amateur of wine. The trouble about the subject is, as readers of *Christie's Wine Companion* will know to their cost, that it does take hold with frightening speed. Paul was meant to represent the typical recipient of our wine course, but soon he was tackling me with tricky little questions such as 'Why exactly is it then that this Vieilles Vignes vineyard of Bollinger's has managed to escape phylloxera?' or 'I thought French barrels were supposed to be best. Why does everyone think so much of Ridge Vineyards if they use American oak?'

The budget, luckily for the six 30-minute programmes and for us, could

Above, Paul Fisher, winemaker Zelma Long and Jancis at the Simi winery in Sonoma

Right, Tasting at Ridge vineyards, Santa Clara

stretch to three forays abroad, to Bordeaux for the vintage, to Champagne for some tramping round the chilly November vineyards and to California for high jinks such as filming in a two-seater plane above Napa and in a refrigerator at the University of California, Davis. In all, it took about eight weeks' filming to come up with the heavily-edited goods, the rate translating into less than five minutes' transmitted film per day of shooting.

I think I was probably prepared for the stately pace at which things are done, or at least achieved, in the film world (the wine world is, after all, not exactly frenetic). What surprised me, however, was how much I *enjoyed* sitting around all day waiting for the light to be just right, the film in the camera to be changed, the aeroplane overhead to have flown out of earshot (a continual problem in California) and my eyeliner to be refreshed. It was rather like spending a whole day in a taxi. You knew you physically couldn't get on with anything else and that there was no possibility of your daydreams being shattered by a telephone. My mind drifted happily along in neutral for hours, only to move up sharply into top gear whenever I was needed on camera. I'm lucky enough to have quite a good memory, so saved the production the cost of a teleprompt.

The hardest part, I found, was interviewing other people. I was already treading a difficult path. 'Oh, you mean claret is a *red* wine?' was only one down from the level of some of the questions I had to use to elicit information from others. Providing the lead-in question to precipitate the desired answer is surprisingly difficult, especially as wine people in general are a loquacious lot, and prone to use an inordinate amount of jargon. 'Riesling. Now that's the great grape of Germany, isn't it?' I found myself interjecting like a half-wit. Michael Broadbent, I may say, is any interviewer's delight. We rarely needed more than one 'take' in King Street; the chap seems a professional at everything, drat him.

Yes they really did say 'Scene 600, Take 2' and clap together the two bits of blackboard on which this was chalked each time before Paul shouted 'Action!' and we lumbered into another scene – though apparently someone has, inevitably, invented the digital clapperboard.

Filmspeak for the group of people working away at *The Wine Programme* on location is 'the unit' (though at times when our three Peugeots were dispersed over the Marne *département* trying separately to find Hautvillers with both walkie-talkies in the same car, I wondered how apt this expression was). Ours usually comprised Paul and myself, plus his assistant, a continuity girl, a make-up girl who spent an *hour* each morning trying to coax my features into some filmable shape, the cameraman, his assistant, a sound recordist and an electrician – and this was considered a pretty small unit. You might think that these technicians, mainly young lads, would be rather thrilled at the prospect of spending a week at Château Margaux, or in Champagne, where they were offered the local wine instead of coffee at 11 each morning. Not a bit of it. They seemed to have just got back from a rum commercial in the West Indies or a documentary about spices shot in Malaysia and China. Wine, it seemed, was very small beer.

It soon became obvious that the 11 o'clock coffee is absolutely vital to the continued output and co-operation of a film crew. One sunny September morning at Château Margaux, on our first day out, the *vendangeurs* almost stopped work in amazement when they saw borne into the vineyard on a delicate gold and tortoiseshell tray from the *château,* nine porcelain cups and saucers with a jug of coffee to refresh the T-shirted band filming their own (much more arduous) activities in the vines.

Sangfroid apart, perhaps the most difficult technique demanded by the business of filming was learning to do 'reverses' when they change the position of the camera so as to train it on the interviewer rather than the interviewee, who then has to repeat all the questions (and in my undisciplined case, exclamations too) so that they can be 'cut into' the original responses. Baron Philippe completely out-acted me when the time came to reverse over his shoulder on to me at his bedside. Never before has a mound of silk pyjama in the corner of a camera frame shown quite so much expression. And the chaps at Marks & Spencer (all of whom seemed to want to be in on the act and refused to nominate a single representative) were disconcerting too. They decided they'd answer all my 'reverse' questions with off-camera teasing, which is why, when I'm supposed to be listening to an outline of their labelling policy, I may have looked curiously mirthful.

Of course it was the process of filming itself that offered all the dramas, such as the three reels of film that the lab (wrongly) reported were 'fogged' and had to be painstakingly shot again, or the cans of sound tape that went missing on the other side of the Golden Gate Bridge. But it was in a scruffy little room in Soho that these miles of plastic tape were fashioned into six entertainments. To take full advantage of the medium, the editor, Andrew Nelson, had to keep cutting from one location to another – though he got no nearer a vineyard than his neighbouring bottling plant at Harlow. Even more complicated was having to include in the final programmes some footage from the pilot film, shot when I was three months pregnant, while the rest had been shot when I was being worn to about half the size by the rigours of early motherhood.

Nor were the problems confined to the visual. Little Julia, aged between ten weeks and five months, was grafted on to the film unit for its travels abroad and at times felt moved to let her mother (and anyone else who might be within a couple of miles) know that she was ready for the next feed. Paul and the rest of the crew were admirably forbearing in this and every other aspect of dealing with me and mine.

Their moment came during our visit to Château Pétrus late one evening as the thrilling 1982 vintage was gently bubbling away in those regrettably few vats. Paul kept on demanding retakes of a scene which had Christian Moueix drawing off a sample of the precious liquid for me to taste – until I whispered to him the approximate price of each glassful. This and other hand-crafted shots meant that poor Christian had to cancel about three later appointments in order to accommodate us (a recurring theme in *Wine Programme* mechanics). As he sat waiting for the final adjustments to be made to the 45-minute business of lighting in a suitably tasteful and subtle fashion, the charming young Moueix managed to beam at everyone, 'How wonderful it is to see others take as much trouble with their work as we do with our wine.' I don't think all of them had tasted Pétrus, but I think they got the point. A premier crew they were.

'. . . And he can pinpoint the exact vineyard just by sniffing the corkscrew'

The Authors

Burton Anderson

a native of Minnesota, came to Europe as a newspaperman in 1962 and began learning about wine from the bottom up with the open whites of Rome's *osterie*. A nine-year stint at the *Herald Tribune* in Paris, punctuated by sojourns in Italy, convinced him that Italian wines were gaining rapidly on French, and if the experts weren't going to tell the world about this renaissance maybe an inspired journalist should. In 1977, he left the *Trib* news desk for his country home in Tuscany to write *Vino*, which won him the 1981 Glenfiddich Award as wine-book author of the year, and *The Mitchell Beazley Pocket Guide to Italian Wines*. He also writes a regular feature in *Decanter* magazine.

Michael Broadbent MW

a Mancunian, though best known for his professional wine activities – tasting, auctioning and writing – has other strings to his bow, being an accomplished pianist and artist – an exhibitor at London's Royal Academy, occasional illustrator and currently chairman of the Wine Trade Art Society whose annual exhibition is held at Christie's. He is founder and editor-in-chief of Christie's Wine Publications, author of *Wine Tasting*, now in seven languages, and *The Great Vintage Wine Book*. His work in the field of wine has been recognised by the French government who, in 1980, gave him the rank of *Chevalier* in the *Ordre National du Mérite*.

Hugo Dunn-Meynell

who was born in 1926, recalls deciding, at the age of eight, what his approach to life would be – to distinguish between the good things (which he intended to enjoy) and the rest, which he would either change or ignore according to his capabilities. He has seen no reason yet to alter this philosophy. The good things have included imaginative cooking, all kinds of wine, travel, and the company of his widely dispersed family and friends. As director-general of the International Wine & Food Society, he has many opportunities for all of these. He is married to Alice Wooledge Salmon, who also contributed to this book.

Patrick Grubb MW

was born in 1932 in Malaya, the son of a rubber planter. He was educated at Wellington College, Berkshire, and was apprenticed in Bordeaux to Sichel & Co, vintaging at Château Palmer in 1973, and studying briefly at Bordeaux university. On his return to the UK in 1974 he worked successively for Hedges & Butler, St. James's Bonded Bottlers, Hay & Son and J. L. P. Lebègue, where he was deputy managing director. In 1958 he became the youngest Master of Wine and 15 years later was invited to become the head of Sotheby's wine department. He is now a director and his interests include collecting wine books and philately. He is married with two sons who are already taking an interest in drinking wine.

Anthony Hanson MW is managing director of Haynes, Hanson & Clark, the London wine merchants formed in 1978 (with the purchase of a wine shop in Kensington) by Denis Haynes, Nicholas Clark and himself. He was born in 1945, and joined the wine trade on leaving Eton in 1963. He worked in cellars in Bordeaux, Champagne and Nierstein, trod grapes in Pinhão, then lived for three years in Beaune. He became a Master of Wine in 1976. His book, *Burgundy*, was published by Faber & Faber in 1982, and reprinted in 1983.

Ian Jamieson MW has been employed in the British wine trade for 25 years. His enthusiasm for wine was aroused at the *Ecole Hôtelière* in Lausanne in 1955 to a point at which he eventually decided to join T. A. Layton in London as a trainee. Besides his interest in wine, he enjoys music (opera, in particular), the theatre, gardening and walking his dogs. In 1970 he became a Master of Wine; he lectures when he can't avoid it, and has served as a trustee of the Wine & Spirit Education Trust. He lives with his family in Kent.

Hugh Johnson was a pupil of the late André Simon, first in 1962 as secretary of the Wine & Food society, then as editor of *Wine & Food*. His first book, *Wine*, published in 1966, is still in print. In 1970 he wrote *The World Atlas of Wine* and each year since 1977 has revised his annual *Pocket Wine Book*. Between whiles he has written a book on trees, *The Principles of Gardening*, and continues to conduct *The Garden* (the journal of the RHS) and its sister-magazine *The Plantsman*. His latest wine book (1983) is *Hugh Johnson's Wine Companion, an Encyclopedia of Wines, Vineyards and Winemakers*.

Max Lake born in 1924, is a former consulting hand surgeon, foundation member of the Australian Hand Club and the author of numerous books on wine. He has been an international wine judge for 25 years. Founder and consulting wine maker at Lake's Folly since 1963, he was the 'first of an entirely new breed of winemaker, revolutionised wine in Australia' (Bradley) and, 'did much for the Hunter Valley, as well as the entire country' (Peppercorn). He has given the André Simon and Lambier Dew orations, is an honorary member of Medical Friends of Wine, a member of the Perfumers' and Flavourists' Association of Australia, and a former chairman of the working party of the National Health and Medical Research Council to revise wine and spirits standards in Australia.

Edmund Penning-Rowsell is wine correspondent of the *Financial Times* and *Country Life*, consultant to the *Good Food Guide* and chairman since 1964 of The International Exhibition Co-operative Wine Society. When Christie's restarted regular wine auctions in 1966, he researched the vast collection of Christie's wine catalogues. From them he picked out items of interest reflecting the tastes and prices of the time, and these have formed the basis of the market reviews in Christie's Wine Reviews. He is the author of *The Wines of Bordeaux* (4th revised edition, 1979). He has been decorated by the French government as *Chevalier de l'Ordre du Mérite Agricole* (1971) and *Chevalier de l'Ordre National du Mérite* (1981).

David Peppercorn MW	has worked in the wine trade for three decades, after reading history and law at Cambridge. Now an independent wine consultant and broker, he is a Master of Wine and former chairman of the Institute of Masters of Wine. He is the author of *Bordeaux*, which won the André Simon Memorial Prize of 1982, and co-author of *Drinking Wine*. His clubs are varied (Saintsbury, Garrick, MCC and the Vintners Company), his interests operatic, and he is married to another contributor to this book.
Sir John Plumb	until recently Master of Christ's College Cambridge, has been the College's wine steward for the last 20 years. He is a founder member of the Bordeaux Club, has been a member of the Saintsbury Club for 30 years, and when not tasting or drinking wine he has devoted himself to the writing of history. He is the author of some 14 volumes, ranging from the Renaissance to the present day but largely devoted to the 18th century.
Jeremy Roberts	born in one of the better vintage years during the war, joined the wine trade in 1961, working in this country, on the continent and in the USA. An early magpie instinct combined with the practical approach to obtain textbooks for his wine trade exams started him on the road to collecting books related to wine. He continues to collect prints and loans them out to the trade in order to fund this favourite hobby. In the meantime he continues to pursue an active career importing wines from France.
Jancis Robinson	is lucky enough to earn her living finding out more about the subject that fascinates her, wine. She is a wine correspondent of *The Sunday Times*, was founder-editor of *Which? Wine* and has written a number of books including *The Wine Book, The Great Wine Book* and now *Masterglass – a Practical Course in Wine Tasting*. As her chapter shows, she has had fun recently finding out about the world of celluloid.
Alice Wooledge Salmon	a native of New York, is the only graduate of Vassar, so far, to have wielded the butcher's cleaver in the kitchens of London's Connaught Hotel. She has the triple profession – based on favourite pastimes – of writer, photographer, and cook, has been a chef not only at the Connaught but at Ma Cuisine, and writes regularly on food, France, and other interests for various British and American magazines. She contributed to Time-Life's *Good Cook* series, and is co-author, with her husband, Hugo Dunn-Meynell, of *The Wine & Food Society's Menu Book*.
Peter Allan Sichel	was born in London in 1931. His British father was of Danish origin, his mother Swedish. Educated in the UK and, during the war, in the USA, he joined the family wine business and for the last 20 years has lived in Bordeaux. Past-chairman of the Bordeaux Merchants Association as well as running Maison Sichel, he looks after the family interests in Château Palmer and Château d'Angludet, also in Margaux, which he bought in 1961 and where he lives with his wife and six children.

| André Simon | the statistics of André Simon's career read like the *Guinness Book of Records*: 67 years of authorship, 104 books, 34 years of active life as president of the International Wine & Food Society after his retirement from 33 years in the champagne trade. At 93, this exceptional wine merchant, author, bibliophile (and in his time, gardener, traveller and many things else besides) remained wise, warm, high spirited; a rare human being. |

| Serena Sutcliffe MW | is a wine broker and consultant, Master of Wine, and author of three books on the subject, the second edition of André Simon's *Wines of the World, Great Vineyards and Winemakers,* and *The Wine (Drinker's) Handbook*. She also writes fiction, and has an unfulfilled ambition to beachcomb. Unfortunately, all the clubs to which she would like to belong (the Saintsbury, Garrick, MCC and Vintners Company) do not accept women members. She is married to a contributor to this book. |

| Bob Thompson | moved from his native Pacific Northwest to San Francisco in 1960, and to the Napa Valley in 1975. He works as a freelance editor and writer on a variety of non-fiction subjects ranging from home building to beachcombing. After writing *The Pocket Encyclopedia of California Wine* (Mitchell-Beazley), *The California Wine Book* (William Morrow, with Hugh Johnson), *American Wine and Wine Cookery* (Meredith, with Shirley Sarvis), *California Wine* (Sunset), three editions of *Guide to California's Wine Country* (Sunset), 38 magazine pieces, 400 newspaper columns, and thousands of tasting notes, he sometimes wakes up in the night wondering if he has become an idiot savant. |

| Harry Waugh | entered the wine trade in 1934, working with Block, Grey & Block until the outbreak of war. After serving with the Welsh Guards, he joined Harvey's of Bristol, where he elevated their fine wine business into the first rank. He now has an active international wine consultancy business, is a director of Château Latour and is responsible for the introduction of the impeccable Classic range of wine glasses. The founder and president both of the English Chapter of *Les Compagnons du Beaujolais* and The Zinfandel Club, he is the author of many books on wine, a regular contributor to international wine magazines and lectures extensively throughout the United States as well as for Christie's recently inaugurated School of Wine. |

| Bernard Martyn Watney | an antiquary and liveryman, he spends his days as an adviser on Occupational Health and Tropical Medicine to a well known British brewery. At night he writes books and lectures on eighteenth century porcelain, wine, wine labels and corkscrews. On the committee of management of a large wine organisation; among his main pleasures are drinking good claret and seeking out little-known wines around the world. |

H. W. Yoxall

was captain of St. Paul's School, London, and a classical scholar of Balliol College, Oxford. He served in the 60th Rifles from 1915 to 1919, and was awarded the Military Cross on the Somme and a Bar to this at Ypres III. He spent his working life in publishing, and was first director, then managing director and finally chairman of Condé Nast Publications Ltd. He was awarded the OBE for charitable and magisterial services.

He is the author of several books, including *The Wines of Burgundy* and *The Enjoyment of Wine*, and of regular wine articles. For the second edition of *The Wines of Burgundy* he was given the 1979 *Prix Littéraire* of the *Confrérie des Chevaliers du Tastevin*, of which he is a *Grand Officier*.

'Why Monsieur, I wouldn't exchange a tankard of home brew'd for a hogshead of claret'
(Thomas Rowlandson)

Editor's postscript

First of all I would like to thank those readers who enabled us to put up the OUT OF PRINT sign so quickly for the first edition of *Christie's Wine Companion*.

I am grateful to several distinguished artists for their contributions – my colleague Michael Broadbent for a glimpse of pages from his now famous notebooks, Charles Mozley for his paintings of Bordeaux châteaux and Merrily Harpur for her drawing on page 198. Pip Youngman Carter drew the portrait of André Simon, and Angelo Cattaneo the map of Tuscany.

I was delighted to reproduce on our endpapers two drawings by Graham Rust from his set of six dinner plates depicting important châteaux in the Médoc. The four châteaux not featured in this book are Beychevelle, Cos d'Estournel, Margaux and Mouton-Rothschild.

Jeremy Roberts, whose collection of rare books is now very impressive, gave me much enthusiastic help and advice. I would also like to thank Sir Kenneth Jacobs for giving me permission to reproduce the Rowlandson from his collection (page 203).

André Simon's chapter on drinking in Elizabethan times, and his description of a memorable meal eaten some 350 years later, both appeared in the *Journal of the Wine & Food Society*. Permission to include the drawing from *Vogue* magazine by Nobili was kindly given by Condé Nast Publications.

I acknowledge with thanks the following who supplied me with the photographs I needed: Alice Wooledge Salmon, ZEFA Picture Library, Il Greppo, Christopher Bradshaw, Emanuela Pellucci, Dr. Bernard Watney, New South Wales Tourism Department, Dr. Max Lake, Hugo Dunn-Meynell, Michel Guillard, South African Farmers Association, BBC Hulton Picture Library, Peter Sichel, Esmond Saqui, Deutsches Weininstitut Mainz and Dennis Davison & Associates. Burdin and I took the photographs of Château Haut-Brion.

Once again I am indebted to Christopher Bradshaw who characteristically gave me much moral support; also to Alison Stanford who, as sub-editor, wrestled with the special requirements of wine writers who do not always agree over certain points of detail. For that reason we have usually followed personal preference – even to hyphens.

Château Lafite-Rothschild